HOW TO ENJOY 1 TO 10
PERFECT DAYS IN
SAN FRANCISCO

HOW TO ENJOY
1 to 10
PERFECT DAYS
IN SAN FRANCISCO

by
JACK SHELTON

NEW AND REVISED

Written in collaboration with
JACK R. JUHASZ

Edited by
DIANE SWEDIN

SHELTON PUBLICATIONS
Box 391
Sausalito, Calif. 94965

Library of Congress Catalog Card Number: 77-75392
ISBN 0-918742-00-5

PRINTED IN THE UNITED STATES OF AMERICA

SHELTON PUBLICATIONS
Box 391
Sausalito, California 94965
(415) 332-1165

Contents

Introduction

Because San Francisco is such a unique and wonderful city, it deserves a unique and wonderful guidebook. I know this book is unique, and I have tried to make it as wonderful as possible.

Since you probably will not be staying in San Francisco for as long as you would like (wouldn't it be nice to have all the leisure time we could ever want?), I wrote this book to give you the best of San Francisco, no matter how short your stay.

The first day, for example, presents what I would recommend to a friend if he or she had only one day to spend in our wonderful city. If my friend had only two days, I would go on to suggest the second day's activities; if he or she had only three days . . . and so forth.

Although the scheduling involves many arbitrary decisions on my part, times and days are set purely as a guide and should not inhibit you. Switch things around to suit yourself.

We begin with suggestions for spending one to ten perfect days in San Francisco. The day-to-day schedule covers one complete, perfect week. For the remaining three or more days, two-, or three-day trips are suggested.

Since dining-out is *the* favorite pastime for native and visitor alike in San Francisco, great emphasis has been placed on restaurant-going in this book. Even though San Francisco is a "restaurant town," it still possesses a substantial number of terrible "tourist traps." To make sure you not only avoid these but discover the truly fine restaurants (many of which do not advertise aggressively), each day's schedule gives you a variety of selections for both lunch and dinner, as well as specific recommendations on what to order. In choosing these restaurants for you, I have drawn on my many years as a restaurant critic for Bay Area residents.

What you will find are 50 of my personal favorites—some famous, others obscure, little "finds"—which will provide you with the finest dining experiences in town. And when that "town" is San Francisco, it means some of the finest dining anywhere! As with your other activities, though, let your personal taste and budget be your guide. If you want to switch restaurant visits around or follow a special craving or whim, do so—I have included a separate restaurant index just for that purpose.

Should you find yourself heading home with a lot left to see and experience, do not feel bad. Remember . . . there is no such thing as visiting San Francisco only once.

JACK SHELTON

PART ONE

One Perfect Week in San Francisco

Your 1st Perfect Day Schedule

8:30 a.m.   Board Hyde Street cable car at Powell and Market Streets in front of Woolworth's.

9:00 a.m.   Arrive at last stop and have breakfast at the Buena Vista Cafe, corner of Beach and Hyde.

10:00 a.m.   After breakfast, stroll to Aquatic Park, the Maritime Museum, Hyde Street Pier, The Cannery, The Wine Museum and Fisherman's Wharf.

11:45 a.m.   Hop a Powell Street cable car and either get off at Pacific Avenue for a "dim sum" lunch at Tung Fong, or the Hong Kong Tea House, followed by a stroll through Chinatown; or remain on board to Market Street and lunch in the breathtaking Garden Court of the historic Palace Hotel.

2:00 p.m.   Pick up your rental car for the 49-Mile Drive, or take Gray Line's City Tour #1.

7:00 p.m.   Cocktails at the Top of the Mark.

8:00 p.m.   A short stroll around Nob Hill.

8:30 p.m.   Dinner at either Jack's, La Mirabelle, La Pantera, or at Maurice et Charles' in San Rafael.

11:00 p.m.   A stroll down "mammary lane"—Broadway —and perhaps a visit to a nightclub.

2:00 a.m.   If you are still up, a goodnight view of San Francisco from the top of Telegraph Hill; or a visit to a "jook house."

How to Spend One Perfect Day
in San Francisco

8:30 a.m. Do not have breakfast (or just have coffee) at your hotel. Find Market Street, which is easy since it is the main thoroughfare of downtown San Francisco, and look for the big Woolworth's store located at the beginning of Powell Street. Right in front of Woolworth's you will find what children and many adults would travel halfway around the world to see—the famous San Francisco cable cars. Board the Powell and Hyde Street one (look for a maroon sign on the roof) and, weather permitting, try to get an outside seat on the right-hand side (Woolworth's side), even if you have to let a car or two go by.

By sitting on the outside section, you will be privileged to watch the gripman as he runs the car. You will quickly discover that cable car gripmen and fare collectors are a breed unto themselves with extraordinarily open personalities. During your over-the-hills ride, you may see them interrupt a flirtation with a blushing, pretty young passenger to chastise an impatient motorist with such remarks as, "You dare honk your horn at a national historical monument?" You cannot help noticing their special pride and warmth about being the ones who give life to "that historical monument," and they will readily answer any questions you may have about the cable car.

However, in case you are shy, let me explain that the cable car runs with the aid of a continuously moving cable (9½-miles-per-hour) located below the street. The street contains an open slot the entire length of the run, and the car has clamps which extend into the slot and fasten onto the cable below to propel the car forward. Releasing the grip stops the car. It cannot back up, but it does have a braking mechanism. In addition, the cable car triggers a device which causes traffic lights on hills to turn green as it approaches. Cross traffic stops so the car can make it to the top. Cable cars contain no electricity and the lights are operated by a battery.

Now, here we go up Powell Street, eight stops to the top of Nob Hill. From your right-hand seat on the cable car, you will get an exciting look down California Street past Chinatown to the Bay. Twisting your neck to look out the other side of the car will show you the famous Fairmont and Mark Hopkins Hotels, both of which you will see more closely later in the day.

Another few blocks—the gripman warns you to hang on as the car first swings left and then soon rounds another curve onto Hyde Street heading toward Russian Hill. Here, the car again starts climbing and in a few moments, you will see two of the most thrilling views in all the world. The first will present itself to you at the top of Lombard Street, "the crookedest street in the world." (Notice how the street curves several times around flower beds.) Your view will be eastward toward Telegraph Hill, capped with Coit Tower, and the Bay with the Bay Bridge connecting San Francisco to Berkeley and Oakland. A quick turn of your head forward and slightly to the left will give you a panoramic view of the Golden Gate Bridge. Then a deep breath as the car goes down the hill—a glance at Alcatraz Island right in front of you and a feeling of relief when the car stops at its final destination, Beach Street. Here you will get off and find yourself in front of the Buena Vista Cafe, 2765 Hyde, (474-5044). It opens at 9:00 a.m. every day, and do not be surprised if you find a line already formed.

9:00 a.m.—Enter the Buena Vista Cafe, find a table overlooking the charming Victorian Park with its cable car turntable and the waterfront beyond, and immediately order (service can be slow when crowded) a fine, hearty breakfast with one of the Buena Vista world-famous Irish Coffees as a finale. Of course, if you have a few encores of this concoction, which was introduced to the United States in 1953 right on this spot, your first perfect day in San Francisco may start and finish at the Buena Vista. However, I can think of worse fates!

To begin your breakfast, ask for another B.V. favorite, their velvety New Orleans Fizz. The rest of breakfast is traditional—eggs with excellent sausage or ham or bacon, served with hashed-and-browned potatoes. Everything is cooked to order, which accounts for much of the often-encountered waits, and the eggs are especially well prepared. The leisurely, mellow Irish Coffee conclusion will make this a breakfast you will long remember, if the mood captures you. And if it doesn't, what are you doing in our wonderful San Francisco anyhow?

I know it might be difficult to think of lunch and dinner right at this moment but in San Francisco, where reservations are required in almost all important restaurants, you have to do just that. My recommendations for lunch give you a choice of two superb Chinatown spots where you can savor delightful dim sum (Chinese luncheon tidbits) in informal atmospheres; or else a feast for the eyes, if not exactly for the palate, in one of the world's most beautiful dining rooms, the Garden Court of the Palace Hotel. You might wish to read ahead for my full descriptions of these unique lunch spots before making up your mind. No reservations are accepted at the dim sum houses but if you opt for the Garden Court, you must call 392-8600 for a 12:30 p.m. reservation before you leave the Buena Vista.

For dinner, I offer four suggestions: the first, La Pantera (392-0170; no reservations accepted), is an inexpensive, family-style Italian restaurant in the North Beach area. The other three are quite expensive. Jack's (986-9854) is a San Francisco institution of over a century which still serves excellent, unfussy French cooking; La Mirabelle (421-3374) is one of the city's finest French restaurants; Maurice et Charles' Bistro (456-2010) is about 25 miles out of town, but it is *the* finest French restaurant in the Bay Area. (Of course, if you wish to try other restaurants reviewed in this book, you will find a complete listing in the special index in the back.) In addition to making these arrangements, if you are planning to drive the 49-Mile Drive yourself, you might wish to telephone your favorite rental car company to make certain they will have a car for you this afternoon at about 2:00 p.m. Once all these necessary phone calls are completed, you can start your walking tour of the Fisherman's Wharf area.

10:00 a.m. When you leave the Buena Vista Cafe, turn left and walk one block down Beach Street. Here you will find Ghirardelli Square, a colorful shopping-dining complex created from an old chocolate factory. Across the street is Aquatic Park and the Maritime Museum (open every day; 10:00 a.m. to 5:00 p.m.). If you have youngsters along, they'll be thrilled with the huge sea anchors and other ocean-going memorabilia on display at the museum; and be sure to show them the intricate miniature clipper ships and freighters. Older folks may want to drop in at the Senior Citizens' Center, located on the lower floor.

After leaving the museum, walk down onto the beach for a view of the Golden Gate Bridge. On the beach, turn right, back toward the Victorian Park and down Jefferson Street. Just past the San Francisco Rowing Club, you will find the Hyde Street Pier (open daily; 10:00 a.m. to 5:00 p.m.; small admission charge). Docked here are five historic ships which you can explore with the aid of by-word headsets. These novel electronic devices enable you to hear prerecorded stories of the ships, as well as wind and weather sound effects. After leaving the Hyde Street Pier, continue down Jefferson Street toward Fisherman's Wharf.

However, before arriving at the Wharf proper, you may wish to take two slight detours. One is to The Cannery, a dramatic dining-shopping complex of unusual design. You can't miss it, for it is on the right-hand side of Jefferson Street as you approach Fisherman's Wharf. The other, situated behind The Cannery on Beach Street between Hyde and Leavenworth, is one of the latest additions to San Francisco's museum scene, The Wine Museum (open from 11:00 a.m. to 5:00 p.m. except Sunday when it opens at noon; closed Monday). Here, in an extremely handsome room, you will find the story of wine—from the growing of the grapes to an incredible display of the Franz W. Sichel Glass Collection, certainly one of the finest in the world. Although sponsored by Christian Brothers, one of California's noted wine producers, the museum is totally lacking in commercialism. After leaving The Wine Museum, head back to Jefferson Street and on to Fisherman's Wharf.

I particularly love the Wharf at this time of day, just before lunch, with its steaming pots of crabs and curbside vendors. If you are lucky enough to be here when the famous local San Francisco crabs are in season, you are in for a real taste treat. Crabs are served in San Francisco all year around but occasionally they come frozen from other areas. The local season usually runs from mid-November to mid-May. The famous San Francisco crab is not to be confused with the smaller, soft-shelled crab of the East Coast. It is closer in flavor and size to the eastern lobster rather than to the eastern crab. The best way to eat our marvelous crab is freshly picked from the shell, sprinkled with lemon juice or dipped into a plain, good-quality mayonnaise.

One of the few San Francisco culinary habits I do not endorse is covering the crab with something called Louis sauce. I have never met Louis but I would gladly strangle him for his creation, which overpowers the crab's delicate flavor. Louis dressing, by the way, seems to be nothing but a diabolic mixture of mayonnaise and catsup. And while at it, I should also like to veto the widespread practice of placing so-called cocktail sauce on San Francisco crab. This strong combination of catsup and horseradish tends to make a soup out of the dish and once again, all you taste is the sauce.

Another seafood delicacy which you will find at the Wharf is the "tiny bay shrimp." Many years ago, San Francisco Bay was filled with delectable little crustaceans very similar to these and thus the name "bay shrimp." However, man's pollution put an end to their being commercially fished. There are high hopes that clean-water ecology efforts will make this feasible again in the future but for today, the term "bay" usually refers to Bodega Bay, waters located north of San Francisco in which these shrimp are found.

By the way, since seafood terminology has never been universally standardized, most local restaurants reserve the term "shrimp" for these tiny crustaceans, and "prawns" for the larger ones. There are no local varieties of prawns; what you find in San Francisco is shipped in from the coast of Mexico or New Orleans, frozen. Our bay shrimp, on the other hand, are fresh—at least those served in the better restaurants which do not cheat with frozen Japanese shrimp —and are available year around. If you want to savor the finest during your stay, plan a daytime visit to Swan Oyster Depot, 1517 Polk Street near California (673-1101). Not a restaurant but a fish market featuring the finest in seafood, Swan serves the ultimate in fresh bay shrimp cocktails from behind an old-fashioned marble-topped counter. Oh, yes, while I strenuously object to the cocktail sauce on crab, I do enjoy it on shrimp. But even then I request it be served "on the side" in order that I may add just the right amount.

At this point, I might tell you about a feud I had with one of our famous local Italian restaurants. The owner insisted upon serving his shrimp cocktails with spoons rather than forks. When I objected, he told me there was too much sauce to use a fork. This, of course, was exactly my point! But plead as I might to use less sauce, he persisted and seems to be doing nicely without my patronage.

Your stroll along Fisherman's Wharf will also introduce you to another San Francisco culinary favorite—our famous sourdough bread. You will spot it either in a heavy, round dome or in a long, cylindrical baton like the traditional French bread loaf. The dome-like loaf has a very hard outer crust with a rather coarse texture inside; the long cylindrical loaf seems to have a softer crust and a smoother inner texture—both, of course, possess a slight sour taste.

Natives continually complain that the sourdough isn't as sour as it once was, which may be true. Nevertheless, it is still one of the world's greatest breads. Oh, if you fall in love with our sourdough and wish to take a "bite" of San Francisco home with you, you will find racks of them at the airport. But we had better be moving on along the Wharf right now.

At the water's edge near Pier 43, you will find your closest, land-based view of Alcatraz. If one of the world's most famous former prisons truly fascinates you (it holds no interest for me), you might want to visit the "Rock." However, reservations for your jaunt to Alcatraz Island, now part of the Golden Gate Recreation Area of the National Park Service, usually must be made in advance for a specific day and time. Sometimes, in the peak visitor season, there can be up to a three-week wait! The telephone number for reservations is 398-1141 and if you do go, dress warmly and wear sturdy walking shoes.

If you haven't seen enough ships at the Hyde Street Pier, your next stop should be further along the waterfront at Pier 43 to board the Balclutha. But keep an eye on your watch; we have a full day planned.

The Balclutha is the last full-rigged ship of the great Cape Horn Fleet. It has been faithfully restored through the generosity of its sponsor, the San Francisco Maritime Museum Association, as well as through contributions from public-spirited San Franciscans, and by members of San Francisco unions who donated thousands of labor hours without charge. Your admission fee goes toward its upkeep.

Although the Balclutha is anchored permanently at Pier 43, it is easy to imagine her anchor is aweigh and you are sailing off in freedom and glory on the world's trade routes . . . for the romantic past of the Balclutha hangs to her from stem to stern. Even the galley and captain's cabin have been restored accurately. If you have any youngsters in your party, looking over every part of this great ship will be certainly one of the highlights of your visit to San Francisco. And even if no children are present, who among us cannot be caught up in the magical daydream of casting off in a full-rigged sailing ship like the Balclutha?

11:45 a.m. Walk three blocks up Taylor Street away from Fisherman's Wharf and you will find the terminal point of another cable car line, the Powell Street line. Board here.

If you have decided on the Chinese dim sum lunch, get off at Pacific Avenue and walk downhill to Tung Fong, 808 Pacific, (362-7115); or the Hong Kong Tea House, 835 Pacific, (391-6365). The former is a tiny hole-in-the-wall while the latter is an enormous palace, very close in feeling to those in Hong Kong. Both are regarded as the finest exponents of dim sum in the city, but because of the Hong Kong's vast size, it does boast a greater selection.

Dim sum, which translates as "heart's delights," are one of the great delights of Chinese cookery. They are little snacks which offer an exquisite array of textures and flavors. If you have never experienced a dim sum lunch, all you need to remember is to remain open-minded and adventuresome! There are no set menus: what you do is hail a tray-laden waiter or waitress and select at random any of the stuffed dumplings, tiny sparerib sections, egg rolls, custard tarts, or whatever else happens to be on the tray. You will then be served a small plate containing two or three portions of each selection. There are no prices; your check will be tabulated by adding up the empty plates at the end of the meal. But let yourself go. Prices are remarkably low and you can eat for hours for under $4.00 per person. Be sure to include favorites such as Chicken in Foil; Char Sil Bow (barbecued pork in a puffy steamed bun); Fon Gor (pink shrimp visible through the thin steamed-dough covering); and Custard Tart for your dessert—each sensational!

After your filling dim sum lunch, a walk through Chinatown before getting behind the wheel of your rented car or in the seat of a tour bus would feel just right. So proceed one block down hill to Grant Avenue, turn right, and you will find yourself in the heart of Chinatown—the world's largest Chinese community outside the Far East. You are

taking your stroll at the best time of day, too, for this is
when the streets are packed with Chinese residents doing
their marketing for the evening meal. Because of the reliance of Chinese cuisine on the freshest ingredients, Chinese
women shop daily in the afternoon. Thus, you will find the
fish markets, delicatessens and green grocers jammed with
shoppers—and I daresay you will be among them, for the
aromas streaming out of Chinatown's markets are simply
enticing! Street scenes in Hong Kong or Taipei are hardly
more colorful or more fun!

Naturally, in between the food shops (the mainstay of
Chinatown's people) are the curio and gift stores. The quality
of wares to be found here range from blatant junk to priceless antiques. During your fourth perfect day, I will devote
a whole morning to Chinatown-shopping but right now, it's
just window-shopping and strolling as you head toward downtown San Francisco.

If you decided not to lunch at Tung Fong or the Hong
Kong but rather at the elegant Garden Court—by elegant,
I mean the dining room itself, not the food—then you can
either get off the cable car at Pacific and take a pre-lunch
walk through Chinatown along Grant Avenue to Market
Street (about nine blocks) . . . or, if you are a little weary
of walking, simply stay on the cable car until it reaches
Market Street. Here, get off and turn left toward the Ferry
Building Tower (you will see it at the end of the street).
Walk about four blocks and you will be at the Palace Hotel,
Market at New Montgomery, (392-8600), with its breath-
taking Garden Court.

The Garden Court was once one of the city's proudest
dining rooms and the hotel itself was called "the world's
grandest hotel" at its opening in 1875. Luckily, we still have
the Garden Court (preserved as a historical monument) to
remind us what hotel architecture was like in that era of
spacious graciousness before the invention of plastic and
neon. And should you be extra lucky in lunching there on
a sunny day with the sun's rays streaming through the high-
glassed ceiling, breaking into rainbow hues as they hit the

prisms of the huge chandeliers, you might believe you are really back in the year 1875.

If the opulent Garden Court has not changed much during this century, its cuisine has—and all for the worse! Yet, localite and visitor alike can still enjoy the magic of this room by skirting the more ambitious luncheon offerings and ordering the famous Palace Court Salad or the Green Goddess Salad. The Palace Court Salad consists of either shrimp, crab or chicken, bound with a judicious amount of mayonnaise, resting atop an artichoke bottom which stands on a tomato-slice base. Surrounding this are lettuce and chopped egg mimosa. "Green Goddess" was the name of a 1915 stage vehicle for actor George Arliss and it was the Palace's chef who invented this now nationally popular dressing as a tribute to the star. Over sixty years later, the kitchen is still turning out a commendable version of this mayonnaise-anchovy-tarragon blend which dresses the lettuce topped with your choice of shrimp or crab in the Green Goddess Salad. The Palace also does well by its pastries and my perennial favorite is the Nut Cupcake.

2:00 p.m. Now it is time to see more of the city. Assuming that your one perfect day in San Francisco will not be too restrained by a budget, I have advised a rather expensive item for this afternoon—renting a car. My reason is the 49-Mile Drive. This driving-tour of the city is a magnificent concept, especially for San Francisco with its incredible views, and the people who conceived the idea certainly deserve the undying gratitude of residents and visitors alike.

The drive is very simple, even if you have never set foot inside the city's limits before, because the route is well marked. All along the 49-mile course are seemingly hundreds of blue-and-white seagull signs indicating the necessary turns and directions. Also, a complete map of the city with the drive clearly outlined is on sale at most bookstores and magazine stands, or available free of charge from the San Francisco Visitors & Convention Bureau Information Center, located in Hallidie Plaza adjacent to the cable car turntable at the foot of Powell and Market Streets. By the way, if you call the Visitors Bureau at a special number (391-2000), you will hear a recording of all important events in the city for that week.

Of course, if you would like to leave the driving to someone else, large comfortable chauffeur-driven limousines are available for less than what you might think from services such as Gray Line Limousines (824-2660). And if you cannot rent a car or limousine, do not feel disappointed in substituting the Gray Line Tour No. 1 of the city which leaves around 2:00 p.m. from their terminal at First and Mission Streets (771-4000). There will be a slight duplication on sights you have already seen this morning, such as Fisherman's Wharf, but certainly not enough to hamper your enjoyment. Since those taking either a limousine or the Gray Line Tour No. 1 will need no further assistance, I will now personally conduct the 49-Mile Drive. Just ask your car rental office how to find the Civic Center.

2:15 p.m. Start at City Hall with its dome towering 308 feet above Van Ness Avenue—over 16 feet higher than the Capitol in Washington, D.C. Opposite it on Van Ness Avenue are twin buildings—the Opera House and the Veteran's Building, both erected in 1932. The Opera House is the hub of San Francisco's cultural life and the home of the San Francisco Opera, Symphony and Ballet. Since its opening night performance on October 15, 1932 of *Tosca* with Muzio, the world's greatest operatic artists have appeared here, many long before setting foot on New York's Metropolitan stage. The opera company normally occupies the house from mid-September to December 1, at which time the symphony takes over for a six-month season.

Next door is the Veteran's Building in which, on its upper floors, is the San Francisco Museum of Art with a permanent collection including Matisse, Picasso, Rivera, and others. However, now is not the time for museum-viewing— I've scheduled that later on in your stay. This afternoon, we just want to get a feeling of the entire city. So off you go up Van Ness Avenue, heading north.

At Post Street, ignore the 49-Mile Drive sign indicating a right turn. That would take you downtown through Chinatown and Fisherman's Wharf, all of which you have visited this morning. Just continue on up Van Ness Avenue, approaching the Bay. At Lombard Street, you will find a large sign indicating a left turn to the Golden Gate Bridge; ignore this also and drive on for three more blocks. (Yes, you will get to the Golden Gate but via a far more scenic route.) At Bay Street, turn left and it is here you pick up the blue-and-white seagull signs which you will now follow for the remainder of the 49-Mile Drive. Bay Street turns into Marina Boulevard and you will soon find yourself along the San Francisco Yacht Harbor, heading toward the Palace of Fine Arts.

The Palace of Fine Arts, designed by Bernard Maybeck, derives its name from the role it played in the 1915 Panama-Pacific International Exposition when it housed the art exhibit. Today, it is the last remaining building of the Exposition. Several years ago, when the Palace was about to fall apart from old age, Walter Johnson of San Francisco donated over $2 million toward its restoration, with the city and state also contributing. Proponents of modern architecture suggested the money be used to tear down the building. San Franciscans were aghast at such an idea, having long treasured the Palace as a symbol of a past era when buildings were created as a feast for the eye rather than solutions to economic and functional needs.

Thus, the Palace of Fine Arts is today as it was yesterday—that is, in outward appearance. Inside, there is a 20th-century museum called Exploratorium. The theme is perception, and there are over 200 exhibits which you can manipulate and activate to make you more aware of your perceptual powers. The Exploratorium (563-7337) is open Wednesday through Sunday from 1:00 p.m. to 5:00 p.m.; Wednesday evening from 7:00 p.m. to 9:30 p.m.; no admission charge but donations are encouraged.

Next, you enter the Presidio, the largest military reservation within a city's limits in the United States. The date —1776—on the gate as you enter is not a mistake because the Presidio served as military headquarters of the soldiers of Charles III of Spain in that year. Later, on your left, you will pass the Officers' Club which is the only, and therefore the oldest, remaining adobe building erected by the Spaniards in San Francisco. Throughout your drive in the Presidio, you will be favored by panoramic views of the Bay and the Golden Gate.

On your left, as you proceed, you will see the National Military Cemetery, significant in that no other cemetery lies within the city limits. Peter B. Kyne, an author, loved to tell the story of how the authorities dealt with his plan to be buried in this cemetery, because it was the only possible way he could be interred within the confines of the city he loved so much. Being a veteran, he went one day to chat with the Commanding Officer, to whom he confided his great desire. When he asked the Commanding Officer if he could reserve a plot, the latter merely glanced at Mr. Kyne and replied in gruff tones, "Mr. Kyne, first come, first served!"

After winding through the Presidio's tree-lined streets, which always remind me of some sleepy college campus of years ago, you will begin climbing up toward the Golden Gate Bridge. However, watch for a sign on the right indicating Fort Point, where you will take a slight detour. Situated at the strategic entrance to San Francisco Bay, the massive brick and iron fort was constructed in 1853, using Fort Sumter as a rough model. Its huge structure is impressive and so are the views of the Bay, the city, and the underside of the Golden Gate Bridge which is high above you. Do not spend too much time snapping spectacular pictures, though, for there are many miles and equally impressive sights ahead. By the way, going at a fairly leisurely pace with several short stops, the 49-Mile Drive takes about 3½ hours.

From Fort Point, retrace your route back up to the main road, turning right. An optional detour is a few yards beyond this turn which would take you to a parking area near the Golden Gate Bridge Toll Plaza. However, I suggest you press on and reserve that stop for a few days later when you go over the bridge.

Again, following the now familiar blue-and-white seagull signs, continue through the Presidio and on to Sea Cliff with its beautiful homes overlooking the entrance to the Bay.

Our drive takes us next to the Palace of the Legion of Honor, an art museum which also serves as a memorial to California's dead of the First World War. There are museums throughout the world with superior collections but few, if any, with a more magnificent setting. You will certainly want to park here and spend a few moments looking at both the Palace itself and the panoramic view it commands.

Returning to the 49-Mile Drive route and proceeding along Geary Boulevard, you will soon find the historic Cliff House on your right—and directly before you, the vast panorama of the Pacific Ocean pounding upon miles of beach. The site of the Cliff House has been the locale for a restaurant ever since 1863 because of its vantage point overlooking the beach and rocks below where sea lions make their home. However, the building which now stands there is certainly not the original. In fact, there have been many Cliff Houses —most of which have been lost to fires. One was even blasted from its foundations when, in 1887, a schooner loaded with 40 tons of dynamite was driven onto the bluff below and exploded. Looking far off to your right, if it is an exceptionally clear day, you will be able to see the Farallon Islands. San Francisco's city limits actually extend 32 miles west into the ocean to include this cluster of islands.

Now, on down the Great Highway, past Fleishhacker Zoo, circling Lake Merced and onto Sunset Boulevard (not to be confused with the neon-jungle street of Hollywood fame) to Golden Gate Park.

How can I characterize this stupendous municipal undertaking except to say that few cities in the world can claim a park within their limits as beautiful and natural, yet entirely man-made! Today, your 49-Mile Drive will take you along most of the park's main drives just to give you a perspective of its beauty and space. However, Golden Gate Park deserves far more than this cursory look and tomorrow, we will devote a whole afternoon to some of its delights, although it would actually take several days to fully explore its wonders. So just relax and enjoy your drive.

After exiting the park, turn right up Stanyan Street . . . then right onto Parnassus Avenue, passing the huge University of California Medical School campus. Then on to Twin Peaks. From its 910-foot summit, the panorama of San Francisco and the East Bay spreads before you. On a clear day, it is one of the most spectacular city views in the world; if it is foggy, you'll just have to buy a postcard of the view back at your hotel. As you drive down Twin Peaks Boulevard and Roosevelt Way, you will catch sight of every conceivable type of architecture in this popular view-conscious neighborhood. Many of the houses perch high atop stilts, craning over the roofs of others for a better view.

Crossing Market Street, your next stop is Mission Dolores, founded by the Franciscan Fathers in 1776 with the historic church dating from 1782. After your visit to Mission Dolores, continue on up Dolores Street. Here you will see a wild assortment of San Franciscan Victorian houses. Recently, it has become the vogue to restore these lovely old residences, but I feel many have gone too far in the use of color, often picking out the ornate wood details in rainbow hues. Nevertheless, they are great fun to see and some are very handsome. Eventually, a left turn onto Army Street will take you into the industrial section of the city and onto one of the freeway routes back towards downtown, passing San Francisco's once-bustling Embarcadero waterfront and historic Ferry Building.

One of the biggest blights on the city's beauty is the overhead freeway above you, which gives a depressing feeling to what could be an inordinately beautiful waterfront. At one time, many movements were afoot to tear down this civic blunder; however, if it still looms over your head as you drive past the Ferry Building, the efforts obviously have not succeeded.

Opposite the Ferry Building is a fine bricked and planted plaza with one of the town's most controversial new landmarks, the Vaillancourt walk-thru fountain. Many hailed its construction as the ultimate in modern design, while others have derided its appearance as something left by a dog with square bowels. You be your own judge! Your route now takes you through the financial district and onto Market Street, where the 49-Mile Drive ends. Find the shortest route back to your hotel for a brief rest and freshening up before hitting the town again for cocktails.

7:00 p.m. To watch it grow dark from the Top of the Mark has been a favorite San Francisco twilight pastime ever since the Mark Hopkins Hotel was built on its choice Nob Hill site. By this time, you should know where the Mark Hopkins Hotel is—you passed within a half block of it this morning on your cable car ride. Even though a dozen skyscraper hotels and office buildings now boast view restaurants and cocktail lounges on their uppermost floor, top honors still go to the Top of the Mark.

Before you select a table, do not hesitate to walk around the room, sampling the 360-degree view of America's most beautiful city. My perennial choice of table is on the west side (to the right as you enter the room) facing the Golden Gate and the setting sun. The Top of the Mark is always crowded and a prime table may be difficult to find; however, you can enjoy some aspects of the view from almost any table.

8:00 p.m. Leave the Mark Hopkins, cross Powell Street and enter the Hotel Fairmont, which boasts what is probably America's most beautiful hotel lobby. In fact, it is one of the few spacious lobbies which has not been converted into a restaurant. Here you may wish to stop for another cocktail or simply stroll around.

The Fairmont was designed by the famous architect, Stanford White, and rebuilt in 1907 after the fire had almost completely destroyed the original structure. (You will note here that San Franciscans prefer to refer to the 1906 tragedy as "the fire" rather than the earthquake. This is to make it clear that most of the damage was done by the ensuing fire rather than by the earthquake itself.)

Leaving the Fairmont, you will see the famous Pacific Union Club across the street. The club's great contribution to San Francisco lies in preserving the only remaining famous Nob Hill mansion, built in 1885 at a cost of over $1.5 million by James Flood who was one of the Bonanza Barons. Today, it stands as a fortress of Republicanism.

Walking past the Flood Mansion and Huntington Park, just across Taylor Street, you will find the imposing and splendid Grace Cathedral. The site, contributed by the famous Crocker family, was once the location of their mansion. The Cathedral houses the first seat of the Protestant Episcopal Church in America.

If the days are long enough, you may wish to wander around the crest of Nob Hill where you will see breathtaking views in almost every direction. The Masonic Temple is here, too, with its surprising wall of "glass" which you can see by peering through the front doors. Although it looks like a huge stained-glass window, the wall is actually a mosaic fused between two sheets of transparent plastic.

8:30 p.m. Selecting where to dine on the first evening in any strange city is always a major decision for me. And reaching my choice of recommendations for you has involved a great deal of soul, as well as palate, searching. This was not true when I wrote the first edition of this guide book over fifteen years ago. At that time, there was no doubt your first dinner should be at Trader Vic's. The Trader Vic restaurant empire was launched right across the Bay in Oakland. But once the San Francisco "branch" was established at 20 Cosmo Place, (776-2232), it became the crown jewel, probably because Vic himself was in residence there. And not only was the food of topnotch quality, but a special room, the Captain's Cabin, soon became the social sanctum sanctorum of the city's elite.

But as the years passed and Vic went into semi-retirement, the cuisine began to develop some flaws, especially when served outside "the Cabin." Therefore, today I can no longer unequivocally recommend my old favorite Trader Vic's to the "unknown" visitor. However, if you happen to be a celebrity of any name recognition or if you have local friends who are "Cabin regulars" and can guarantee you entry into this vastly enjoyable room, dinner at Trader Vic's can still be a memorable experience. Yet, even in the Cabin I would restrict my ordering to the simpler, unsauced dishes (particularly those from the Chinese oven) and avoid the more ambitious preparations. Also in the Cabin, I strongly recommend you request the assistance of one of the captains in ordering. They are among the finest in town, thoroughly versed in the kitchen's output and on exactly how to pamper the most pampered international celebrities and local luminaries. Oh yes, don't be bashful in ordering one of Vic's justifiably famous rum concoctions—even the natives do!

If you are seriously interested in cuisine and are looking for the best, here are four different restaurants from which to choose for your first evening of San Francisco dining.

Actually, my first recommendation is not located in San Francisco but rather in Marin County. It is called Maurice et Charles' Bistrot, 901 Lincoln Avenue at Third Street in San Rafael, (456-2010; reservations imperative). Dinner here, though, is only possible if you have retained the car you rented for this afternoon's 49-Mile Drive. San Rafael is about 25 freeway minutes from downtown San Francisco. (Cross the Golden Gate Bridge; follow the main highway to San Rafael. Take the Central San Rafael exit, keeping to the left so you can make the first available left onto Third Street. Continue on Third for three blocks, then right on Lincoln. Maurice et Charles' Bistrot is on the corner.)

Here you will find an elegant bistrot—graffiti-scrawled-on whitewashed walls, wine glasses larger than soup bowls, and a madly mod mixture of patrons comfortable in anything from levis to black tie. But far more important is the food— the ultimate in French cuisine. Created by a young chef from Lyon, the offering is very limited and changes season- ally, as it should in any great French restaurant. One item which is a mainstay, though, is the quenelles, cumulus clouds of poached fish dumplings bathed in a cognac-enriched sauce. Also, the bistrot's terrines of sole or salmon are not to be missed when available.

Lamb is one of the West's best meats (veal can be risky in all but the very finest restaurants) and Maurice et Charles' treatment of tenderly pink slices wrapped in flaky pastry tempts customers time and again. Pureed vegetables, such as artichoke, along with a brilliantly green spinach timbale usually garnish the almost overly indulgent plates. You might wish to cleanse your palate with a crisp green salad and some cheese before proceeding to a dessert of made-on-the-prem- ises sherbets and ice creams. Consider yourself extra blessed if the evening's selection happens to include either their banana or incredible fresh blueberry spiked with cassis! The wine selection is limited and therefore only barely ade- quate for this class of haute cuisine. Expensive, as you would expect for the very best.

If you are interested in fine French cuisine but have not rented a car or are turned off by a 25-minute freeway drive, then I would recommend La Mirabelle, 1326 Powell Street near Broadway, (421-3374; reservations imperative). While Mirabelle's decor will never make *Architectural Di- gest,* the cuisine is certainly of award-winning caliber. Cervelles au Beurre Noir, calf's brains of a delicate quasi- custardy texture sauteed in browned butter and dotted with capers, is an ideal opener. Mirabelle also can conjure up exceptional quenelles, placing a close second to those of Maurice and Charles'. My favorite main course at Mirabelle is the Poulet Grand'mere, a rustic casserole-roasted chicken made the more flavorful by the inclusion of onions, chunks

of bacon, carrots and celery root. Sensationally succulent!
Also ask about fresh fish preparations, unlisted on the menu.
A crisp green salad would then set the palate for one of
Mirabelle's expert souffles or made-to-order Tarte Tatin,
that caramelized upside-down apple tart heaped with fresh
whipped cream. Other baked desserts are from Fantasia,
San Francisco's premiere bakery. Expensive.

Still French but less fancy than either Maurice et Charles'
or La Mirabelle is Jack's, 615 Sacramento Street near Montgomery, (986-9854; reservations imperative). Jack's is a
San Francisco institution of well over a hundred years. The
great-grandchildren of San Francisco's finest families today
dine at their ancestral tables. But do not expect anything
elaborate at Jack's. Its decor is men's room lighting and
plastic palms; its cuisine, however, is honest, unfrilly, basic
French.

The menu changes daily but if today happens to be a
Saturday, do not miss the ambrosial sorrel soup. Their rack
of lamb, crispy outer crust and meltingly pink within, is always served with potatoes boulangere—an unbeatable combination. Also try a side order of their deep-fried eggplant
or zucchini. For dessert: any fresh berries or melon in
season; or their incomparable French Pancakes, not the
gussy overly sweet things known as suzettes, but rather
simple little crepes. The coffee, served in cafeteria-style
crockery, is just about as bad as anywhere in town, which
points up San Francisco's major culinary flaw—uniformly
poor coffee. Nevertheless, if I were forced into exile and
had to leave my beloved San Francisco, my last meal would
be the above described feast—not only because it is so
superb, but also because it is served at Jack's. Expensive.

Now, don't think just because all the above recommendations are on the expensive side that I am going to ignore
the budget-conscious visitor. Not at all. My next choice is
La Pantera, 1234 Grant Avenue near Vallejo, (392-0170).
La Pantera is not just a restaurant; it's a happening. Located
in the heart of San Francisco's North Beach area, La Pantera is the finest remaining example of that uniquely Italian

dining experience—the trattoria. At La Pantera, modern amenities such as credit cards, reservations and private tables are scorned. You sit at communal tables of eight or more, rubbing elbows with struggling students, tough truckers, Brooks Brothers businessmen and their denim-clad dolls, or even a society dowager. The service is strictly family style— a platter or two of each course is plopped onto the table and the rest is up to you. It's a great way to meet real San Franciscans. Table talk is usually food oriented, although when I was there on the night of the Patty Hearst conviction, a brawl almost ensued when the "self-appointed jurors" retried the trial. But all this tells you nothing about the food.

Well, a typical dinner is a homemade Italian soup, perhaps a clear broth with pastina or a joyously fresh minestrone. Then some type of pasta or stuffed zucchini. (Saturday is traditionally ravioli night and La Pantera's are just about the best restaurant ravioli in town!) Then roast beef or roast chicken or chicken cacciatore or whatever the kitchen comes up with . . . and whatever that may be, you can be certain it will be plentiful, piping hot and beautifully prepared. Plus, there always seems to be side orders of favorites such as garlic-tanged, sauteed Swiss chard or even fresh boiled tongue in a tomato sauce. Someone at the table must be delegated to mix the salad dressing for the fresh green salad. Dessert is always fruit and cheese. The cost? Under $6 per person, including a small bottle of wine which makes La Pantera just about the greatest dining-out value in the United States!

11:00 p.m.   San Francisco nightlife is just about beginning at this hour so if you have traveled to San Rafael, head back to town, turning right down Van Ness Avenue and then left onto Broadway. If you stayed in town and dined at either Mirabelle or Pantera, Broadway is only a block away. If Jack's was your dinner choice, take a cab to the corner of Broadway and Columbus. A stroll down Broadway, or as some call it, "mammary lane," is taking in a part of San Francisco's recent history. This gaudy three-block strip is where topless and bottomless entertainment all began. An ersatz commemorative plaque on the side of the Condor, *the* home of it all, attests to this dubious distinction. Every year, the street becomes more honky-tonk. Nude encounter sessions, porno movies and you-get-what-you-pay-for come-on's all ply their trade here. However, now that porn and topless are no longer the exclusive property of "Sin City," one wonders what Broadway will turn to next.

One nightclub which has survived years and years of change on this street is the internationally famous Finocchio's. Finocchio's presented "drag" shows long before the word came into vogue. (Its more genteel translation is "female impersonators.") The lavishly costumed entertainers put on a tongue-in-cheek show which would hardly shock your maiden aunt from Oskosh. But if you do visit this San Francisco landmark, be prepared to find busloads of conventioneers in the audience.

In San Francisco, "name" entertainment always play the Venetian Room of the Fairmont Hotel. Joel Grey, our own Carol Channing, Tony "Left-My-Heart-Here" Bennett and other friends make annual visits. For a more comprehensive listing of nightclubs, check the night-life section of the Sunday newspaper or *San Francisco Magazine,* available at most newsstands.

2:00 a.m. After the first edition of this guidebook appeared many years ago, my telephone rang about 2:05 a.m. The voice on the other end was that of an obviously inebriated woman. "Mr. Shelton," she slurred. "I love your guidebook and have been following your suggestions all day. But it's now two in the morning, all the places have closed and you have no more suggestions. What should I do?" I told her as gently as I could to go to bed, and the next day my phone number became unlisted.

However, for those of you still up, I have a couple suggestions. True, San Francisco, even with its overblown wicked reputation, does close up pretty tight at 2:00 a.m., the official "last call for alcohol" hour. Years ago, there were all sorts of places you could go to hear great jazz and drink watered-down scotch out of cracked coffee cups. But they are all gone—or at least that's what my cabbie-spies tell me. And even if they weren't, I couldn't recommend them in print—otherwise they would be gone for sure! So, how about taking a cab or the car if you have it, and driving up Telegraph Hill to Coit Tower—the remarkable edifice fashioned after a fire hose nozzle as a tribute to our fire fighters by Lillie Hitchcock Coit—for a good-night look at the lights of San Francisco below you. It's only a few minutes from Broadway.

If you are hungry again, you can go to a jook house: Sam Wo Company, 813 Washington Street off Grant Avenue, (open until 3:00 a.m.; closed Sunday). "Jook" is a type of Chinese rice gruel, served so piping hot that when you drop in your choice of raw beef, chicken, shrimp, fish, etc., it cooks almost instantly. My favorite is the one with fish; be sure to order a Chinese Doughnut with your gruel. I also enjoy their delicious Raw Fish Salad, Won Ton soup, and Beef-Tomato Soft Noodle Chow Mein. Sam Wo absolutely abounds in local color. Very inexpensive.

3:00 a.m.   Good Night!

Now, if your plans provide for a longer stay in San Francisco, I shall take you through the second day of your one perfect week.

If not, you are now wiring your boss, telling him that this is the greatest city you have ever seen, and he simply must permit you to stay for the rest of the week or month. (The author assumes no responsibility for his reply!)

So, read on to begin your second perfect day.

Your 2nd Perfect Day Schedule

9:00 a.m.   Breakfast at Sears'.

10:00 a.m.   Shopping tour of downtown San Francisco.

12:00 noon   Lunch at either Plum or What This Country Needs.

1:00 p.m.   Drive or take easily accessible public transportation out to Golden Gate Park. See the Flower Conservatory, de Young Museum, the Asian Art Museum, the Aquarium and Planetarium, or just stroll.

4:00 p.m.   Tea at the Japanese Garden.

4:30 p.m.   Climb Strawberry Hill or feed the birds on the edge of Stow Lake.

5:00 p.m.   Back to your hotel to freshen up for dinner.

6:30 p.m.   Stroll through Ghirardelli Square and have cocktails overlooking the Bay at Senor Pico's.

8:00 p.m.   Dinner at Ghirardelli Square either at the Mandarin, Modesto Lanzone's or Paprikas Fono.

10:00 p.m.   A nightcap at the Buena Vista Cafe? Or just straight to bed . . . it's been a long day!

The Second Day of Your
One Perfect Week in San Francisco

9:00 a.m. There are many world travelers who will rush to Sears' at 439 Powell Street near Post, (986-1160) for their first breakfast during each San Francisco stay, as quickly as others rush to the Top of the Mark for cocktails. Little wonder, for where in the world will you find your plate shimmering with 18 pancakes (small, thank goodness) crowned with whipped butter and maple syrup? And along with them, you can order excellent ham, bacon, link sausages or the very special smoked country sausage patties made especially for Sears'.

Breakfast to many (and possibly this includes you) is the most important meal of the day. Sears' meets the challenge with distinction. Begin with an all-fresh Fruit Cocktail instead of the traditional orange juice which, even here, is frozen. Then proceed to the famous pancakes; or to eggs beautifully cooked accompanied with crispy hash browns; or to a distinctive French toast made from San Francisco's famous sourdough bread. Then split an order of their baked-on-the-premises Coffee Cake to top it all off. Closed for dinner but fine lunches are served until 3:00 p.m.

10:00 a.m. You now find yourself in a perfect strategic position for a morning of shopping, serious or "window" variety. Whether you want to look for some personal needs which you neglected to pack, gifts for those back home or possibly for your host and hostess in San Francisco, or just splurge on yourself, Union Square is the place to start. Simply turn right for a half block when you exit Sears' and you are at the entrance to Union Square. Walk through the Square diagonally—dodging the pigeons and panhandlers—and as you come out, you will see across the street your first stop, I. Magnin's.

I. Magnin and Company: By virtue of location, exterior and interior decor and merchandise, I. Magnin rules the retail scene in San Francisco with few to challenge its austere position. A simple elegance pervades its main floor with not-so-simple elegance on the price tags. However, do not let this frighten you, particularly if you are in the market for gifts. As with any fine shop, there are many small items in excellent taste at moderate prices. Although it is noted primarily as a women's apparel shop, do not overlook its men's department on the ground floor, and a truly superior gift gallery on its 8th floor.

Macy's: If you exit Magnin's by the main entrance on Geary, turn left to enter Macy's just up the street a bit. Should you choose the Stockton exit, turn right and Macy's is just next door. Although an associate of the famous chain, Macy's San Francisco is as different from New York's 34th Street jammed store as night is from day. Merchandise, however, is comparable and medium-priced. Selection, as with all Macy's stores throughout the country, is extensive, and variety is the keynote. Don't miss the recently added Cellar, an innovative concept wherein the entire lower level is treated like a European street, with each section simulating a separate shop. It is mainly devoted to cooking equipment and luxury foods, but also includes books. And if your breakfast is wearing off, stop for some of Fantasia's cookies at the Bakery Shop or a snack at Mama's Restaurant.

Liberty House: Leave Macy's by the Stockton Street entrance and directly across the street is Liberty House, a branch of the Hawaii-based specialty chain. Especially noteworthy is that it kept the famous old Normandy Lane Basement—one of San Francisco's leading sources of luxury foods and cooking equipment—when it bought out the Lane's former operators, the City of Paris.

Joseph Magnin: Directly across O'Farrell is this chic, "with-it" shop, primarily fashioned for women's clothing needs, although it does have a good men's department, as well.

Prices tend to be less stratospheric than I. Magnin's. Incidentally, despite the name similarity, there is no connection between Joseph Magnin and I. Magnin.

Time to make a critical decision: You are presently at a geographic spot where you can go one of two ways. Do you want to throw caution to the wind and splurge? If so, reverse your direction and head back to Post Street, above Union Square, for the posh shopping area. If not, continue one block down Stockton to Market Street, taking in Grodins, Roos-Atkins, the Emporium and ending at Woolworth's. Well, no matter what you decide, here are some capsule descriptions taking in both directions.

Grodins and Roos-Atkins: Across Market Street from one another are these two men's specialty stores; however, they do carry women's wear, as well. Prices are reasonable but large selections are the keynotes. And Roos-Atkins has the added attraction of having in its basement an extensive sports shop.

The Emporium: Market, between Fourth and Fifth. Aptly named, this is the largest store in Northern California. With the conversion of most San Francisco department store basements to gourmet centers, the Emporium's is the last remaining vestige of that heritage of earlier retail tradition, the true "bargain basement."

Woolworth's: Market and Powell, just across the street from the Emporium, it is one of the nation's largest Woolworth's. Actually, this San Francisco branch is more than a store— it's a carnival! Here you will see orchids and pizza sold a few steps from each other and you may hear a demonstrator shout out praises for the latest gadget designed to revolutionize your life. There is even a fancy food department with such rarities as canned buffalo meat and genuine Swedish hardtack.

Back at Union Square: You will discern a trend which is providing the Square with a kind of international flavor. As retail stores become more and more expensive to operate, only the most successful and long-established can afford the rents. As a result, two types of businesses are buying up most of the prime retail space in San Francisco, as is the case in most other large cities: one being banks and the other, airlines. Fortunately for Union Square, as each retailer gives up the ghost, the valuable space is gobbled up by an airline. Because of the airlines' interesting displays, featuring exotic places to see, their windows give the Square an international flavor.

Bullock and Jones: Facing Union Square on Post Street is this attractive building, reminiscent of fine old British establishments devoted exclusively to men's apparel for the older man or the conservative younger one. They have a superb collection of fine English shoes. Exiting Bullock and Jones, turn left down Post to Stockton, turning left again to inspect the charming Ruth Asawa fountain on the steps of the Hyatt On-Union-Square Hotel with its intricate details of San Francisco scenes.

The Tailored Man: Stockton Street, across from the Hyatt Hotel. In sharp contrast to nearby Bullock and Jones, this lively shop features at surprisingly reasonable prices the very latest men's styles, greatly influenced by European high fashions. And if you cannot find what you want, European-trained craftsmen will make a custom-tailored suit for you from a large selection of imported fabrics. Ask for either Tony or Peter, two unusually talented and knowledgeable clothiers. Also, do not overlook their excellent custom-made shirts.

Scheuer Linens: Immediately next door to the Tailored Man on Stockton. Long-established and reliable, this is where countless San Francisco families obtain luxurious linens for dining room, bath and bedroom. Many imported items are available here and nowhere else. (NOTE: If your shopping list includes extensive buying of linen or bedding, especially in unusual sizes, also check *Lenore Linens,* 498 Jackson, 421-6756.)

Alfred Dunhill, Ltd.: On the corner of Post and Stockton is the formidable local branch of this world-wide purveyor of cigars, pipe tobacco and leather goods, along with a small selection of men's clothes. (NOTE: For the pipe devotee, many visitors to San Francisco swear by the mixture sold by mail throughout the world at the *Jim Mate Pipe & Tobacco Shop,* 575 Geary, 775-6634.)

Gumps: Just a few doors further down Post Street from Alfred Dunhill's you will find what is probably San Francisco's most internationally known shop, and for good reason. Although its early reputation was gained by its priceless jade collection and some of its merchandise is still on the expensive side, it has introduced many items of good taste at amazingly reasonable prices. It is one of the best gift shops in San Francisco and certainly a place which deserves your attention if you plan to take gifts home as a reminder of your trip. You can browse through Gump's at your leisure, and you should not miss the jade collection on the third floor, or the limited but fine collection of lithographs and paintings. Gump's also offers a topnotch framing service.

Elizabeth Arden: Should any women visitors require "touch-up's" during their stay, this branch of the international chain is conveniently found in between Gump's and Abercrombie & Fitch.

Abercrombie & Fitch: What can be added to the fine reputation of this great sports center? This branch is a worthy sister shop to the famous one in New York and features everything from a tennis ball to a boat.

Shreve's: Corner of Post and Grant. The Tiffany of the West Coast, or perhaps it is true, as some San Franciscans maintain, that Tiffany's is the Shreve's of the East Coast. Either way, this is for you if you love the beautiful in china, sterling, and jewelry.

Malm Luggage: Before continuing straight down Post Street, you may wish to detour a bit. Turn left and cross Grant

Avenue to inspect this leading luggage and leather goods shop. Always on hand is one of the widest selections of functional, as well as beautiful, French Luggage made in California and sold in the nation's luxury stores. They also maintain a fine repair service, to which they can direct you in case of need.

Podesta Baldocchi: In between Malm's and Tiffany's is one of America's most famous florists. If you have a more than average interest in flowers, especially unusual species, ask to go downstairs to the workrooms. And should you come to San Francisco anytime between Thanksgiving and Christmas, don't miss their display of tree decorations. Even natives stand in line to view them.

Tiffany's: A very small version of the original in New York, but you can easily spend just as much money.

A. Sulka & Co.; FAO Schwarz; Mark Cross: Back on Post Street and to your left, you will find this miniature reproduction of New York's Fifth Avenue.

Brooks Brothers: Diagonally across the street—back in the direction from which you came down Post Street—is staid, old Brooks Brothers, a branch of the distinguished New York shop. Their windows, which look as if they have not been changed since 1818, give many devotees a warm feeling that old values never die.

S. Christian of Copenhagen: Next door to Brooks and occupying several floors, here is a gift and house-need shop, stressing the Danish look.

Saks Fifth Avenue: If you are not yet ready for lunch and the shopping bug is still firmly entrenched, reverse your direction, turn right at Brooks Brothers onto Grant Avenue, cross Maiden Lane and there you will see Saks. Although threatening for years to move into a new building on Union Square, such plans have been delayed and may not have reached fruition by the time you read these words.

Maiden Lane: An almost private street which stretches for only two blocks in either direction from Saks, featuring a wide variety of colorful shops.

Helga Howie's: Probably the most traditionally popular stop on Maiden Lane, this brown brick building with its small, tunnel-like entrance is the only shop in San Francisco, and one of the few in the world, designed by Frank Lloyd Wright. It may surprise you to notice that although built in 1949, it uses the exact principle which is still startling New York today at the Guggenheim Museum, also designed by Wright. The building, however, is not the only beautiful thing about Helga Howie's. This distinctive women's shop is known for its stylish clothes, especially knits.

Robison's Pet Shop: Frisky puppies often play in the windows of this established firm, and sometimes youngsters are lucky enough to see a monkey there, too. Many years ago, the Robison family owned a food store near the waterfront. Sailors, then deprived of fresh food on their long sea voyage, came in and often bartered exotic birds and other pets for fresh edibles. Soon, the Robison's saw more potential in pets than food and hence, San Francisco's leading pet shop came into being.

Now, Maiden Lane returns you to Union Square: You can call it a day—of shopping, that is—or you can continue your exploration of San Francisco via its stores. Should the latter be your choice, either right now or later during your stay, here are a few more noteworthy places:

Wilkes Bashford, Ltd.: 336 Sutter. This store is similar to the Tailored Man but more luxurious, as are the prices. It features Polo clothing for men by Ralph Lauren, which it has exclusively in the city.

Williams-Sonoma: 576 Sutter. One of the nation's finest culinary shops, with the ultimate in functional and decorative items for the preparation and serving of foods. Ask if they will have any of their helpful cooking demonstrations during your stay; admission is free, and famous cooks and writers are guest teachers. Also be certain to request your name be placed on their mailing list for their superb catalogue; there is none finer in America today.

Sherman Clay: 141 Kearny. This music emporium contains everything from a bongo drum to an organ. It is one of a chain of over 65 Northern California and Northwest music stores and enjoys a reputation unequaled in its field. (NOTE: The Sherman Clay store at Sutter and Kearny Streets also sells tickets at regular prices to most leading San Francisco classical musical events.)

Marsh's Oriental Art Co.: 522 Sutter. If this is your interest and you are in the area today, you will be glad to know that Marsh's is among the few dealers in oriental *objets d'art* and antiques *not* located in Chinatown. (NOTE: For shops in Chinatown, see the morning schedule of your fourth perfect day.)

Anthony's Shoe Repairing Shop: 54 Geary. Not only is this store famous for top quality shoe and handbag repairing while you wait, but also for its outstanding shoe-dye facilities. They will even mail their work anywhere in the country.

12:00 noon After a morning of shopping, it would be wise for you to lunch downtown so you will be fairly close to your hotel, to which you can return for a rest prior to our afternoon activities in Golden Gate Park. This day, as with most days of properly seeing any city, involves a considerable amount of "on your feet" activity. Thus, midday rests are good investments for maximum enjoyment.

If your memories of restaurants in department stores are none too happy, little wonder. For all too many years, these eateries have set forth shop-worn chicken salads, as if the ladies would not accept anything more substantial. But today, things are looking up, perhaps because of women's lib. And in the Normandy Lane basement of Liberty House, O'Farrell at Stockton, you will find a marvelously creative place simply called Plum, (772-2242).

Although an adjacent stylish cafeteria shares some of the menu items at slightly lower prices, the attractive art-deco aura of Plum more than compensates for the nominal increase. Etched-glass panels break up the large space into more intimate and comfortable sections, while rich browns and natural woods mitigate any possible sterile feeling and provide a restful oasis from the shopping area bustle. Soups, served in miniature kettles, are represented by a robust onion plus a consistently topnotch soup du jour. Omelettes and salads are distinctively delicious. In the latter category, there are two outstanding attractions—a rarely found, truly authentic Salade Nicoise; and an even more unusual Chilled Julienne of Beef. Among the outstanding hot dishes are calf's liver served with avocado (a seemingly incompatible marriage which ends very happily); beef bourguignonne; and stuffed eggplant. Desserts are the only letdown on an otherwise distinguished menu: The cheesecake with strawberry sauce is not overly sweet and much above average; and the Fortnum and Mason's Plum Pudding is always reliable. Your choice of seven teas or cafe filtre concludes a pleasantly restful lunch. Typical Plum touches such as their use of sweet butter and unusually fine French baguettes, give this charming room a decidedly European flair. Moderate.

Should you prefer to spend less on lunch, or if your shopping tour has taken up more time than it should and you want to press on, my alternate recommendation is equally convenient, located in the Hyatt On-Union-Square Hotel at Post and Stockton Streets. It is called "What This Country Needs" (398-9220) and is not a five-cent cigar but rather an incredibly successful restaurant operation.

A few years back, obviously taking their cue from Campbell Soup commercials, many restaurateurs turned to luncheon places featuring soup. A whole raft of them opened within a two-year time span and the best was and still is What This Country Needs. Service is cafeteria-style; you sit at tables supported by shapely manikin legs, which cause some controversy. But no argument is made over the quality of the soups served. Each day, three different varieties are available and their culinary range is global—for example, an almost ebony, sherry-laced Cuban Black Bean; a creamy, lemony Greek Avgolemono; a vegetable cornucopia called Zuppa Italian Antica; a paprika-accented Hungarian Goulash, etc. To help you decide your selection, a sign above each kettle gives you the full list of ingredients.

A generous bowl of soup, aided and abetted by a chunk of good, crispy French bread, is an appetizing and inexpensive lunch. However, if you crave more substance, the sandwiches are above the lunch-counter variety and happily, half sandwiches are available. You might also consider giving in to the tempting dessert selection—the Banana Chocolate Pie is beautiful!

1:00 p.m. And now for an afternoon in the park—San Francisco's inimitable Golden Gate Park. There is no need to take your rental car, if you still have it, because the park can be easily reached by public transportation. The only necessity one must take is comfortable shoes, since seeing and feeling the beauty of the park is best experienced on foot.

For those wishing to drive, however, simply head out Geary Street. At Geary and Gough Streets, on your left, you will see St. Mary's Cathedral, seat of the Roman Catholic Archdiocese of San Francisco. Although many have been critical of its architectural design, likening it to the agitator in a gigantic Maytag washing machine, I find its clean lines of white marble enormously impressive. Continue along Geary watching for signs which indicate "Masonic Avenue, Right Lane." Take this exit, turning left onto Masonic and following it to Fell Street. Turn right on Fell, first bearing to the left and then to the right as you enter the park proper. The sign here reads "To Ocean." This places you on John F. Kennedy Drive and in a few seconds, you will come to our first stop, the Flower Conservatory which is on your right.

Now, let me allow those of you who are coming by bus to catch up. To reach Golden Gate Park by bus, simply

walk down Stockton Street to Market. Board either a
Hayes #21 or McAllister #5 bus which will eventually take
you along Fulton Street, the northern boundary of the park.
Leave the bus at Arguello Street and enter the park, keeping to the right. Continue to John F. Kennedy Drive, then
turn left and you will quickly find yourself in front of a
huge, ornate greenhouse, the Flower Conservatory.

The Conservatory is the oldest and most charming building in the park. It is a copy of the famous Kew Gardens
near London and was originally designed for the private
estate of James Lick near San Jose. Mr. Lick died before
he could add this dazzling building to his collection. When
the executors of his estate placed the materials for sale, a
group of San Francisco citizens donated the purchase price
and offered the materials to the park for erection.

Professional botanists may be disappointed because the
Conservatory's collection of flowers and plants is not comparable to the great collections of the world. However, it
does house a beautifully arranged and pleasing display.

Enhancing its tropical collection, which includes a pool
filled with water lilies of great size, is the Conservatory's fine
assortment of hybrid orchids. Plus, the exhibition room in
the west wing is changed almost monthly, featuring the outstanding blooms of the season. Many San Franciscans make
it a point to visit this room with each change. We are told
that all of the plants shown in the Conservatory are grown
in the park's own nursery and none are obtained from the
outside.

As you leave the Conservatory to return to Kennedy Drive,
you will want to stroll among the outdoor flower beds, where
you will also note a special display which usually spells out
words of greeting to visiting organizations or proclaims civic
fund-drives. The Conservatory is one of the city's show-
pieces which draws as many residents as out-of-town visitors.

To leave the area in front of the Flower Conservatory,
cross Kennedy Drive by taking the underpass walkway,
which places you on the south side of the thoroughfare. Turn
right on exiting the tunnel and continue along the paved

path marked "bike route." Soon you will find yourself in a small grove of giant ferns, enormous leafy plants with an otherworldly quality to them. Your walk also will take you past the entrance to the John McLaren Memorial Rhododendron Dell, marked by a small statue of the "creator" of Golden Gate Park. The dell itself is a 20-acre triangle, devoted almost exclusively to the park's most popular flower. If your visit to San Francisco just happens to be around late April, you must allow yourself a few minutes to investigate this incredible collection of hundreds of rainbow-hued varieties.

Continuing on past the entrance to the Rhododendron Dell, you soon reach (on your left) the entrance to a large complex of buildings, surrounding a music concourse with a band shell at the far end. This is the hub of the park's indoor activities. Circling the music concourse are:

The M. H. de Young Memorial Museum (directly to your right) which houses masterworks by El Greco, Rembrandt, Hals and Gainsborough, as well as America's Gilbert Stuart, John Singer Sargent and Thomas Eakins. Eighteenth-century French paneled rooms, complete with their priceless furnishings, have been installed in one area; while in another, you can view the traditional arts of Africa, Oceania and the Americas.

The Asian Art Museum: *The Avery Brundage Collection* is a two-story wing of the de Young, although it operates independently. The Brundage is one of the greatest collections of the art of oriental civilizations; I personally have only seen finer in Taiwan. For anyone interested in blue-and-white porcelains, jade and the other exquisite art forms developed centuries ago in the Orient, this museum is an absolute must!

California Academy of Sciences, directly across the concourse from the de Young, consists of a triumvirate of buildings housing an aquarium, halls of science, and a planetarium. Most impressive, to me, is the Steinhart Aquarium in the center with its 14,000 plus living aquatic habitants.

If today is blessed by San Francisco's typical benign sunshine and the idea of walking miles of museum corridors does not appeal to you as much as the sight and scent of newly cut grass and blossoming flowers, I will not blame you for by-passing these fine institutions for another visit on perhaps a more conducively foggy or rainy afternoon. However, we have allowed suffcient time in this area for at least a short visit, so you might use the time to rest your feet by sitting in front of a great master canvas.

If you want to look at more in the museums, don't try to "crack" all of them in a single day. The human eye cannot take in that much. So be selective—perhaps just sample the Brundage or visit my favorite El Greco. Today, we want to simply get the feel of this time and place in this park. You can always come back tomorrow or even on your next trip. After all, the object with sightseeing anywhere in the world is not to see how much you can see, but how *well* you can see it. And if your interests lie in the tremendous wealth of art, history and all aspects of nature and mankind which these buildings offer, you might wish to make a mental note to schedule a return visit sometime later in your stay.

4:00 p.m.   And now what would be more appropriate after viewing the wonders of nature in the Rhododendron Dell and the Flower Conservatory and the wonders of creative man in a museum, than to see them brought together in harmony in the magic of a Japanese tea garden. Japanese garden designers, artisans of the highest order, have a unique way of working with nature. In densely populated Japan, where land is at a premium, these geniuses are able to convert the smallest spaces into miraculous retreats where one can contemplate nature. Unfortunately, the serenity of a Japanese tea garden can be upset by vast hordes of camera-toting visitors brought in by polluting buses . . . and this often happens at the Japanese Tea Garden in Golden Gate Park.

Yet, since it is late in the afternoon, hopefully the buses

have pushed on and you can wander at will through the little pathways which wind in and around such delicately refreshing beauties as golden carp swimming in still ponds or tall bushes forever moving with a quiet breeze which seems to be everywhere in this precious garden.

And, if you are lucky enough to be in San Francisco during the early spring (from the end of March through April) the blossoming trees make the Tea Garden even more magical. Well, no matter when you visit, you will want to savor more of its Japanese flavor by making a short stop at the little tea house, where you will be served by authentically garbed Oriental waitresses. Only tea and a few Japanese cookies are available. And be certain to take all the leftover cookies with you; you will be needing the crumbs in a few minutes.

4:30 p.m. Leave the Japanese Tea Garden through the main entrance and turn to your right. Continue walking along this path, which follows the wall of the Tea Garden, and soon you will come to a flight of cement steps. Climb these and walk directly ahead to Stow Lake.

Stow Lake is the largest lake in the park, and presents a scene of beauty and of people enjoying nature. Along its perimeter, you will see young and middle-aged joggers puffing along, elderly people in conversations with "park acquaintances" with whom they probably have shared the same bench every sunny afternoon for years, and children squealing with glee as they feed the geese, ducks and other water fowl who make Stow Lake their home. Be a child for a moment, yourself, and offer the birds the crumbs from those Japanese cookies.

In the center of Stow Lake, you will see a small island called Strawberry Hill, accessible by two bridges. The top of this hill was once one of my favorite places in the entire city. Years ago, a 75-foot waterfall, Huntington Falls, used to cascade down from the top. And on climbing up, there used to be a rustic bridge made of what seemed to be wood and stone. Closer examination, however, showed that there was no wood at all but rather cement covering wire mesh. These are now gone but Strawberry Hill is still worth a climb.

No matter which way you turn once you are up there, beautiful San Francisco presents herself. Also, because it takes some effort to reach the top and because the hill itself seems to be a "secret place" for many people, those that do come here seem to be extra friendly. And as you walk up the steep slope, you might find a student reading a text or a young couple sunning. Invariably, they say a quiet hello in recognition that you share their place.

If you do not think you want to make the effort to climb up, perhaps you can read about the park while you rest alongside the shore.

Unlike most city parks which were merely shaped out of existing woodlands, the entire area of Golden Gate Park used to be little more than sand dunes swept back from the Pacific Ocean beach, with no lakes and practically no vegetation. This great park, in all its apparent natural variety, was constructed out of 1000 acres of barren land. But do not think that everybody applauded the attempt. There were those who were skeptical and ridiculed the planners. They doubted the possibility of growing trees and grass on hills of sand which were constantly changing shape under driving ocean winds. But the miracle was accomplished!

Under the direction of William Hammond Hall, Park Superintendent in 1871, the first control of the sand was begun. Small boys were paid to go into the hills and collect seeds from wild plants which could grow in sand and provide anchorage.

In 1890, John McLaren became head of the park and remained so right up until his death in 1943. So great was his fame and his equally great contribution to the development of the park as we know it today, that many books on San Francisco have erred in crediting him as sole creator of this park raised out of sand. Though the original concept of Golden Gate Park was not Mr. McLaren's, its creative growth and brilliant nurturing were, for 53 years, in his hands. And it is because of him that Golden Gate Park has no "Keep Off the Grass" signs. With the exception of newly seeded areas, every nook and cranny of the park is open to the public.

Because every bit of vegetation you see in Golden Gate Park had to be cultivated and brought in from elsewhere, the park today houses what is probably the largest variety of trees and plants from all over the world ever assembled in a city park. The only varieties missing are those which have defied all possible attempts at growth in this climate.

And speaking about defiance, if you climbed up Strawberry Hill, you have seen . . . sand dunes. The sand is coming back since the waterfall no longer flows. Indeed, man may exert years of hard labor to fashion nature to his will, but nature is patient and will slowly work to reclaim what is hers. With man's neglect of his beautiful but artificial waterfall, nature stepped right back in. With wind and rains, she slowly began to eat away the topsoil covering which man had brought in, thereby revealing the real composition of the park—the enormous sand dunes that were there long before any of us.

5:00 p.m. Now, it is time to head back to your hotel. If you have come by public transportation, all you need do is walk to Fulton Street, the north boundary of the park, and board a McAllister or Hayes Street bus which will take you back downtown to Market Street. If you have driven to the park, simply retrace your steps back to your car, parked in front of the Flower Conservatory. Right behind the Conservatory, you can exit the park onto Arguello Boulevard; turn right onto Geary, and you are on your way to downtown San Francisco.

Note: You will notice that throughout this book, you are given drive-yourself and bus transportation directions. However, you can certainly substitute taxis. San Francisco has many taxi cab companies, all charging the same rate. For the best service, my personal preferences are the De Soto Cab Company (673-1414) and Luxor Cabs (673-4040).

Be forewarned, though, that cab fares in San Francisco are probably among the highest in the nation. Of course, if you have ridden taxis in New York City, you may be glad to pay the extra charge in return for the warm courtesy for which San Francisco cab drivers are well known. They still tell the story of the New Yorker who fainted when a San Francisco cab driver thanked him for a tip, only to be revived and then faint again when the same cab driver opened the door and helped him out with his packages!

In fact, this might be a good place to stop and talk about courtesy, because it is one of the first things visitors notice about San Francisco. Naturally, San Franciscans are human, too, and there are exceptions. But, by and large, San Franciscans are among the most polite people in the United States, and certainly the friendliest. This means that even if you are visiting here alone, you probably will enjoy your stay more than you would in most other cities. Do not be surprised if the very proper-looking lady sitting next to you on the cable car or in the cafeteria starts a conversation. And, of course, do not hesitate to start one yourself.

If you find yourself standing on the outside of one of our cable cars with an armload of packages, the lady or gentleman seated in front of you most likely will insist on holding the packages for you. This is common custom here and you should not refuse the invitation although, like most visitors, you may find it a bit startling at first!

6:30 p.m. Most American cities, especially tourist-conscious ones, have some kind of historic edifice which has been converted into a shopping-dining complex. San Francisco has two exceptional examples within a few blocks of one another—The Cannery and Ghirardelli Square. The latter, which happens to be my favorite, was designed as a factory complex in 1893; and for 70 years, this 2½-acre site was the home of the Ghirardelli Chocolate Company. When the chocolate makers moved, the massive brick complex could have been leveled to make way for another high rise for the well heeled. But thanks to civic-minded William Matson

Roth, the ancient buildings marked by the quaint clock tower, curiously a copy of the Chateau Blois in France, were converted into a warren of shops and eateries, opening onto a sunny piazza with another capricious Ruth Asawa fountain. As I understand it, the original shops and restaurants came to the square by invitation only. Shops range from quality imported gourmet items, exotic kites, handcrafted jewelry to the finest in Scandinavian household items, all in good taste.

And good taste is also a product of several of the square's many restaurants. For this evening, I offer three of its best for your selection. Not only does this array present an ethnic kaleidoscope—Chinese, Italian and Hungarian, a mini-example of San Francisco's envied cosmopolitan culinary heritage—but all of them also offer Bay views. However, in case you may not be among the lucky patrons to obtain a prime table at one of these restaurants, I have solved the problem by suggesting you have pre-dinner drinks at Senor Pico's handsome cocktail lounge from where you can take in the activity on the Bay through huge tinted windows. But try to resist any hors d'oeuvres since a multi-coursed dinner awaits you. (Again, I am assuming you have read ahead, made your selection, and called for reservations.)

8:00 p.m. Dinner at The Mandarin, Modesto Lanzone's, or Paprikas Fono.

The Mandarin, Ghirardelli Square, (673-8812; reservations advised), is probably the most beautiful Chinese restaurant in San Francisco. And to knowledgeable restaurant-goers, it is much more than that. Before Mme. Chiang opened her original Mandarin in a small cubbyhole far removed aesthetically and physically from this sumptuous site, San Francisco knew little of Chinese cooking other than Cantonese. In fact, just about 99% of all Chinese restaurants in America were Cantonese. Today, the Bay Area hosts hordes of restaurants devoted to the cuisines of Peking, Szechwan, Hunan and Shanghai; and invariably, you will find in their kitchens a Mandarin "graduate." Yet, to me, The Mandarin still retains its unrivaled preeminence.

And the best way to enjoy its superb cuisine is to ask to speak to either Mme. Chiang or her knowledgeable manager, Mr. Lin Chien, when you call for your reservation. Indicate that you are seriously interested in the finest in Chinese cuisine and wish assistance in planning your dinner. The Mandarin can be the most exciting restaurant experience in San Francisco and it is well worth this extra effort.

To help you order, here are some favorites: Chiao-Tzu, meat-filled steamed dumplings crisply fried on one side; Scallop Soup, a marvelous blend of flavors and textures; Smoked Tea Duck; Velvet Chicken, a melt-on-your-tongue blend of chicken breast and egg whites; Mongolian Lamb, shredded lamb barbecued on a special grill and served in wallet-like buns; and for dessert, Glazed Bananas with a hot syrup coating which crystallizes when the bananas are dunked into ice water. You also may be interested in requesting a Szechwan dish which, with its spicy hotness, will make any Tex-Mex chili seem cool in comparison. The Mandarin is one of San Francisco's greatest restaurants with prices to match.

Modesto Lanzone's, Ghirardelli Square, (771-2880; reservations imperative). I like Modesto Lanzone's although I realize it is not a *great* Italian restaurant. But then, San Francisco has no truly great Italian restaurant. There are some fine trattorias such as La Pantera which was recommended last night, and some superb Neapolitan pizzeria-restaurants such as Tommaso's which we will get to later on. However, possibly because San Francisco lacks the requisite top quality milk-fed veal, great Italian cooking just does not seem to thrive here.

At any rate, this shortcoming can be skirted easily at Modesto Lanzone's by starting your dinner with their superb Insalata di Mare, a memorable mixture of bay shrimp and squid, marinated in a tangy vinaigrette. Then look to the pastas. No other restaurant gives you such an incredible array—linguine, agnolotti, panzotti, fettucine, tortellini, gnocchi. If

I order the linguine (specially requesting it be "al dente" which literally means "to the bite"), I usually opt for the marinara sauce. All too often, American Italian restaurants mercilessly overcook their tomato sauce to an acid bath. But Modesto's is sweetly fresh and ideally seasoned. The panzotti is more exotic—spinach-ricotta cheese squares in a creamy sauce crunchy with minced walnuts. And naturally, with San Francisco's Genovese colony, no Italian restaurant here can avoid pesto, that ambrosial basil-garlic-cheese sauce flavoring a fine plate of fettucine. For dessert: fresh fruit or Sacripantina, that sinfully rich cake also from Genoa. Fairly expensive.

Paprikas Fono, Ghirardelli Square, (441-1223; reservations for six or more only), is a small piece of Hungary transplanted to the third floor of the Cocoa Building. Mr. and Mrs. Fono have not only accurately re-created the food of their native land but the delightful spirit and decor of a Hungarian inn, as well. Naturally, you cannot pass up the native dish, Gulyas—a boldly red soup, thick with cubes of beef and potato, sprightly seasoned with paprika. Order some Langos with it and show your gastronomic savvy by rubbing these unsweetened crullers with raw garlic. As a main course, the Chicken Paprikas is succulent boned chicken breasts in a satiny paprika sauce served with the classic galuska, mini-dumplings similar to Swiss spaetzle. In contrast, the Casino Supper proves the Hungarian superiority in frying chicken. There are all sorts of tempting side dishes: Fresh Beet Salad and the ubiquitous Hungarian Cucumber Salad. But you cannot leave Paprikas Fono without having some dessert, so save room. And for dessert, try the Walnut Palacsintas to discover what Hungarian crepes are all about. Stuffed with pureed walnuts, these delectable pancakes are bathed in an ebony chocolate sauce. Wow! Or try Paulette's Torta, an almost sour chocolate cake of devastating richness. For a wine, there is Hungary's Egri Bikaver, bull's blood. Moderately priced.

10:00 p.m. After a full day of window-shopping and park

strolling, I would not imagine you would desire anything other than a comfortable bed right now. However, if you still feel like "going," the Buena Vista is only a block away and you might want to drop in before boarding your cable car to take you back downtown. Have an Irish Coffee for me!

Your 3rd Perfect Day Schedule

9:00 a.m. Breakfast's at Mama's on Nob Hill.

10:00 a.m. Drive or take a bus to the Golden Gate Bridge for a short stroll on the world-famous span.

10:45 a.m. Continue on, either by car or bus, to picturesque Sausalito with its dramatic view of San Francisco.

12:30 p.m. After a walk through Sausalito, lunch at either the quaint Soupcon or on the spectacular outdoor terrace of the Alta Mira Hotel.

2:00 p.m. Off to marvelous Muir Woods, natural habitat of our famed giant redwoods.

4:00 p.m. Drive back across the Golden Gate. If you took a bus over, you can now enjoy an early cocktail on the ferry as it carries you back across the Bay to San Francisco.

6:00 p.m. Rest at your hotel or write those postcards—now or never!

8:00 p.m. Dinner at Schroeder's, that bit of Bavaria by the Bay, or at the exotic Moroccan El Mansour.

10:00 p.m. Since you are in casual clothes, why not dance your ass off at a disco of the same name?

The Third Day of Your
One Perfect Week in San Francisco

9:00 a.m. If today is not a Monday, our plans are to leave town. This delightful little trip will enable you to see at very close hand the Golden Gate Bridge (in fact, you will cross it), the unique hillside town of Sausalito with its intriguing shops (many of which close on Mondays) and sweeping panorama of San Francisco, and the giant redwood trees of Muir Woods. It is a trip you can make by car or a combination of bus, taxi and ferry boat. So while you enjoy your breakfast at Mama's, read on and decide how you will travel, and do not forget to make the necessary reservations.

Mama's at Grosvenor Towers, 1177 California Street at Jones atop Nob Hill, (928-1004), is the ideal spot for a leisurely breakfast. First of all, the restaurant is spacious yet maintains a cheerful intimacy with flower-bedecked dividers and latticed gazebos. Secondly, Mama (Sanchez) is a stickler for the highest quality, as your breakfast will bear out. Freshly squeezed orange juice is a rarity in San Francisco, but not at Mama's. And while her "M'omelettes" are popular favorites, I find her imaginative French Toast to be her greatest breakfast offering. Invariably, I order the version using a highly flavored Swedish cinnamon bread and request the optional topping of fresh, in-season fruit—a marvelously sunny combination. Her Eggs Bentley, fluffy scrambled eggs seasoned with sauteed onions, are in the Rolls-Royce class but unfortunately, the coffee is that non-vintage beige brew which San Franciscans keep tolerating year after year. I can't understand it. Anyway . . .

10:00 a.m. Breakfast over; let's begin our trip. First, let me give directions for those wishing to drive. After leaving

Mama's, drive out California Street (away from the Bay) to Franklin (one block past Van Ness Avenue) and turn right. As you proceed down Franklin, you will pass a few choice examples of Victorian homes, such as the Haas-Lilienthal House at number 2007 on your left. Built in 1886 in the Queen Anne style, it survived the '06 fire and is now open as a museum (Wednesday, Saturday and Sunday afternoons only; admission charge). Another beautiful example in the Italianate style is on the far right corner of Franklin and Pacific. When you get to Lombard Street, turn left and proceed to the bridge, turning right into the "View Area" immediately prior to the toll plaza.

The Golden Gate Bridge was, for many years, known as the longest single-span suspension bridge in the world—4,200 feet between its towers. However, its length is not the chief reason for its fame. Other cities may build larger bridges or taller ones, but I doubt if they will ever build a more beautiful one. For to do so, they would have to match the setting—the beautiful coastlines on both sides, the majestic hills of Marin on the north, the city of San Francisco sparkling like a jewel on the south. They would have to build a machine to create great billowy banks of fog for stunning visual effects. They would have to make certain their calculations produce a graceful, simple and noble shape. And then they would have to paint their bridge red, a daring move which is usually a great surprise to visitors who see it for the first time.

And so, if the Golden Gate Bridge has lost its title as the longest single-span suspension bridge in the world, it has not lost first place for grandeur and beauty.

Incidentally, if you simply must have statistics, here they are: The Golden Gate Bridge was first opened to pedestrian traffic on May 27, 1937, when 202,000 people thronged across it. The next day, vehicular traffic began. The bridge is 8,940 feet long and its pillars tower 746 feet above high tide. At the center, you find yourself 220 feet above low water which explains its attraction to suicides. The tops of the towers rise above the water approximately the same height as a 65-story building. But there are no statistics for the hours of pleasure it has provided both visitors who gasp at its breathtaking beauty upon first seeing it, and residents who cross it twice a day but never seem to tire of its beauty.

If there are children in your party, you now have an excellent chance to enjoy one of the delights of San Francisco while at the same time help your youngsters blow off steam—you can walk across the Golden Gate Bridge to the view area on the Marin County side. (Note: If your party is split between the younger and older generations, part of your group may wish to drive the car across, meeting the walking contingent at the lookout point on the other side. However, please be warned that it is a long walk and you are not advised to attempt it unless you are dressed warmly and have a good deal of stamina.)

10:45 a.m. After taking your fill of the sweep and majesty of this awe-inspiring structure and the fresh ocean breeze in your lungs, it is time to proceed to our next destination— Sausalito. Simply drive across the span and take the Alexander Avenue exit to the right. The long downward drive from the highway into Sausalito is a beautiful one. On one side are the grass-covered, rolling hills of Marin, seemingly far removed from urban life; while on the other, you can catch glimpses of the towers of downtown San Francisco. A "Slow to 15" sign alerts you to the fact you are entering Sausalito. And slowing down here is a good idea for it will also enable you to view the variety of houses perched on the hills above you. Up there, real estate prices are as spectacular as their picture-window views. Find a parking space in one of the side streets near Second and Main Streets (watch for the big Valhalla restaurant sign on your right), while I escort those coming over by bus.

If you are making the trip by bus, after leaving Mama's simply cross California Street and hop a cable car going west. Get off at Van Ness Avenue, the end of the line, and walk one block to your right to Sacramento Street where you will find a bus stop (green, red and blue sign) for the

Golden Gate Transit (call 332-6600 for schedule information). Note: The Golden Gate buses are not part of the
San Francisco Municipal bus system, so you should be
looking for the ones which are predominantly white and
green, bearing the same tri-color insignia as the bus stop
sign. On boarding the bus, ask the driver to let you off at
the Golden Gate Bridge toll plaza so you can view the bridge
as did those going by car.

If you wish to walk across the span, you can do so and
pick up a bus to Sausalito on the other side. However,
because of the location of the bus stop on the Marin County
side, you will be walking a good two miles. If you do not
wish to make this trek, simply return to the spot where you
got off and catch the next bus for Sausalito, asking the driver
for the Second and Main Street stop.

Whether you came by car or bus, you are now at Second
and Main. You will want to walk from here down Main
Street to take a peek into Sally Stanford's famed Valhalla
restaurant, colorfully furnished with a wild assortment of
turn-of-the-century bric-a-brac. Thousands of words have
been written about Sally Stanford and her unique checkered
career. Years ago—World War II days—the name Sally
Stanford was synonymous with San Francisco's shady night-
life; she was the proud madam of the town's most elegant
bordello. Later, Sally went "legit," and opened the Valhalla
in Sausalito. Probably as a tongue-in-cheek reminder of her
past, a red light always burns in an upstairs window. Then,
in 1975, Sally Stanford achieved what she had been trying
to do for many years—she became mayor of Sausalito. I
like to think that Sally and her career could only happen
in places like San Francisco and Sausalito.

On the Bay side of the Valhalla, you will find a colorful
seaside boardwalk which will lead right into Bridgeway, the
main street of Sausalito. Strolling along Bridgeway towards
the business district is a lovely walk. That rock on your
right in the water which resembles a sea lion is not, as many
visitors think, a natural phenomenon shaped by the sea into
a likeness of the animal—but rather, it is a stone carving.

At just about this point, a glance up the hill on your left will reveal a house looking somewhat like the truncated foundation for a fortress. Had not the indignation of some townspeople been brought to bear upon William Randolph Hearst, Sr., the building might have been completed and Sausalito could very well have been the possessor of the famed castle, San Simeon. But Mr. Hearst was invited to leave town by a delegation of husbands and fathers at the insistence of their wives who disapproved of Mr. Hearst's moral standards.

Those of you who came over by bus will have to decide on which side of Bridgeway to walk. On the left are dozens of little shops, cluttered with the latest fashions, handcrafted jewelry and the most unusual in antiques. On the right are intrepid fishermen hoping to pull something from the lapping Bay waters. Those of you who drove over will have to return to your car by the same route, so you will be able to cover both sides of the street.

Soon you will come upon the town square with its two unusual and somewhat incongruous elephant statues to greet you. These elephants and that nearby fountain were originally part of the Panama-Pacific International Exposition held in San Francisco in 1915, and were donated to the city of Sausalito after the close of the Exposition.

Almost across the street is the Village Fair, a "must-see" for any visitor. The structure was an abandoned garage until it was converted into a showcase for several independent little shops. It is sort of a mini-Ghirardelli Square, although many years older. The Village Fair shopping complex was a natural for Sausalito, since the town was long famous for its local craftsmen and artisans. It is a totally delightful maze and don't hurry through—there are many things to see (and buy!).

12:30 p.m. For your luncheon spot today, I am going to give you two choices and your decision will depend on your tastes in food as well as the weather. If good food is your prime requisite (as it is mine), then I suggest a tiny hole-in-the-wall called Soupcon, which has about eight tables (reservations imperative!) and is frequented almost exclusively by natives. However, if the weather is balmy and the view of San Francisco too magical to resist, I recommend the deck of the Alta Mira Hotel. Let me tell you a little more about both places.

To reach Soupcon, continue walking north on Bridgeway after leaving the Village Fair. When you come to the first traffic light (at Johnson) turn left one block, passing the fire station. Then turn right on Caledonia. You will find Soupcon on the corner at 49 Caledonia Street, Sausalito, (332-9752).

If you pronounce Soupcon as most Americans do— "soup's on"—you have an important clue as to what you should order. Its clothes-closet sized kitchen concocts some of the finest and most offbeat soups I have ever savored. Consider yourself doubly lucky if the day's offering includes: Crab Bisque, chunks of fresh crab (still in the shell) in a homemade, fresh tomato bisque; Chicken and Avocado, a surprisingly tantalizing partnership; or Potato-Onion, unlike almost any other elsewhere. Soupcon's sandwiches are equally unique with a breadless Dorothy Cousins, named after a Soupcon "regular" who is as totally delightful as her sister, Julia Child. Another favorite, the Jack Hammer, is sliced baked ham blanketed with melted Monterey jack cheese on a French roll bed, garnished with fresh fruit. Desserts are as acclaimed as Soupcon's soups and equally wild. For example, try the mind-blowing combination of chocolate cake with a cheesecake filling, aided and abetted by blueberries. Truly, a rare luncheon experience—from beginning to end!

A sunny lunch on the terrace of the Alta Mira Hotel, Sausalito, (332-1350) can also be an experience—that is, from a charming, open air, panoramic point of view. However, the food at the Alta Mira appears to have been steadily declining over the years. The Coquette Salad which, a decade ago, I termed an "excellent dish" is now barely passable. The salad consists of enough lettuce to feed a rabbit hutch, topped with mediocre sliced turkey, and sparsely garnished with fruit. As for the cooked dishes, I can no longer tolerate them. Nevertheless, the view is truly magnificent and the decision is yours.

To reach the Alta Mira, climb the staircase marked Excelsior Lane, located next to the Wells Fargo Bank opposite the town square. The entrance to the hotel is at the end of the shaded lane.

2:00 p.m. It is now time to quit basking in the sun of the Alta Mira deck or chasing the last crumbs of your Soupcon dessert, and head on to the Muir Woods National Monument. Again, allow me to give directions to those going by car. Retrace your steps back along Bridgeway to your car; then drive through the town, heading north. The mountain top you see ahead of you is Mount Tamalpais (2604 feet). Muir Woods is located at the bottom of its southern slope. As you are exiting Sausalito, follow the sign indicating Highway 101—Eureka. Then take the first turnoff which is marked "Mill Valley, Stinson Beach, Route 1." Route 1 soon begins to cut through eucalyptus groves and curves over the rolling hillside. You will leave Route 1 at a turnoff marked "Muir Woods 3 miles."

If you do not have a car, there are three other means by which you can reach Muir Woods. The Gray Line (771-4000) runs daily bus tours from San Francisco to the woods, passing through Sausalito on the return trip. This would not be useful today, since we want to spend time at the Golden Gate Bridge and walking around Sausalito. The second way you can reach Muir Woods is by taking the Golden Gate Transit Bus #60 from Sausalito which operates twice a day on weekends only (call 332-6600 or 453-2100 for current schedule). It represents a great savings over the last alternative—which is a taxi—but because Sausalito is usually quite jammed with visitors on weekends, I feel you would be more comfortable if you avoided all that jumble and came over on a weekday, excepting Monday, of course. The Sausalito Yellow Cab Company (332-2200) does run a special taxi service to the woods. The fare is about $20 and includes the round-trip cab ride, along with approximately 45 minutes at the park. But whether you go by bus on the weekend or cab during the week, you *must* go to Muir Woods.

Named in honor of the famed naturalist-conservationist-writer, John Muir, Muir Woods is the closest refuge to San Francisco of the giant sequoia, the redwood—the world's tallest living thing. Every great city has its so-called tourist attractions. These are usually termed "must-see's." In fact, I myself used that term a few pages back. However, Muir Woods is not just a "must-see," it is a "must-experience." I don't imagine many San Francisco residents spend a morning or afternoon going through Muir Woods on their own. Yet, it is amazing how eagerly they will volunteer to show visitors this beautiful oasis. Like residents of all cities, I guess we feel somewhat self-conscious about frequenting sightseeing spots. But just provide the excuse and I, for one, would be glad to spend many quiet hours in Muir Woods.

Naturally, the main attraction is the redwood tree, that unbelievably tall and majestic creation of nature. Although not the largest in the West, the ones which you are looking at rise an impressive 250 feet or more and reach a diameter of 17 feet. To see these trees would be reward enough, particularly at a point so close to the city of San Francisco. But Muir Woods offers more than this. It offers a natural habitat for the redwood—an exquisite atmosphere of surrounding companion shrubs which have remained faithful to these great trees for centuries.

Take time to walk back into the woods a ways. You will be surprised how quickly you can detach yourself from the hubbub of an arriving busload, most of whom head straight for the gift shop. Walk back along the trail and find yourself a rippling brook and drift with its mellow sound for a while. Here, to me, the towering trees impart a cathedral aura, and the silence stemming from it truly creates a religious appreciation for life. If you want to ponder the insignificance of man, just sit quietly and consider the fact that some of these trees were already alive before Christ.

Also, while we are in the park, I think it appropriate to mention how thankful we should be to our national park service. The way in which they have carefully, but unobtrusively, marked out the paths and sights of interest—including the Miwok Braille Trail for the blind—hints at what government *can* be capable of accomplishing for the people.

4:00 p.m. If you came by car, you can experience the park as long as you wish, at least until sunset which is the closing hour. However, for those of you who came either by cab or bus, it is now time to leave. By automobile, simply exit from the park following the well marked signs back to San Francisco. Your taxi or the Golden Gate Transit bus will take you back to Sausalito's town square. Here, you should check the ferry schedule posted at the ferry dock on the Bay side of the town square (or telephone 453-2100) for the next departure to San Francisco.

If, during the day, you have envied those who were able to travel by car, you should feel much better making your way back by ferry. For while they are driving the 17 freeway miles back to San Francisco, you can relax on the upper deck of the ship, a drink in one hand (cocktails are *de rigueur* on the Bay for many ferry commuters), tossing potato chip crumbs to the hovering gulls with the other. And the Bay at this time of day can be fantastic. For those of you who cannot make the ferry trip today, I have scheduled a Bay cruise for later in your week. No matter how you manage it, a trip on San Francisco Bay should not be missed.

On docking at the San Francisco side, adjacent to the historic Ferry Building, you might wish to walk across the Embarcadero and drop into the Hyatt Regency Hotel. If you have never seen one of these incredible multi-storied Hyatt lobbies, this is an awesome example—complete with fountains, huge sculptures, and elevators of Buck Rogers design. You might wish another cocktail in the revolving

Equinox Room at the top. Then, it is either a cab or public transportation back to your hotel.

6:00 p.m. I am certain a couple hours of rest after your long day would be welcome right now. Back in your hotel, you can catch the evening TV news and find out what the world has been doing, or write those postcards—it's now or never!

8:00 p.m. Tonight's dinner selections are both very casual (in fact, in one place you nearly sit on the floor and eat with your bare hands) and both are moderately priced— but they are as different as can be. Schroeder's, 240 Front Street near California, (421-4778), is a vast German beer-hall-restaurant serving hearty meat-and-potato fare accompanied by overflowing steins of beer. The menu, which changes daily, is chalked onto blackboards strategically mounted throughout the cavernous room. However, I never have to check them to see if my favorite first course is available, as it is a mainstay—Herring in Sour Cream. Schroeder's does their own marinating in the cellar and the result is impeccable. For main courses, the Baked Chicken, German Style is a delicious dish of chicken parts atop egg noodles, smothered in a cheese-glazed cream sauce. After hiking through the woods, it is appropriate stick-to-your-ribs food. Other specialties are: Koenigsberger Klops with Sauerkraut, light German meatballs in a caper sauce; Roast Loin of Pork, moist and tender in a way that appears easy for German cooks. The Wiener Backhuhn, pan-fried chicken, also can be extraordinary provided you make the waiter swear it will be cooked to order. And don't miss the Blueberry Square for dessert. Beer, steins and steins of it, should be your beverage. A bit of Bavaria by the Bay at very moderate prices.

If you are in the mood for something far more exotic and do not mind a lengthy car, bus or cab ride, then I recommend El Mansour, 3123 Clement Street at 32nd Avenue, (751-2312; reservations imperative). By car, simply drive out either Geary or California Streets to 32nd Avenue. From Geary, turn right one block to Clement; from California, turn left one block. Since Moroccan dining is more than just a pleasure for the palate but rather a multi-sensory experience, I strongly recommend you take along two necessities. The first is a completely open mind, one that will not hamper your enjoyment of eating the food with your bare hands; in keeping with the true Moroccan dining experience, forks and knives are not presented. Your open mind also will help open your palate to such flavor marriages as cinnamon and sugar used to season chicken, in addition to the heady accents of cumin. The second requisite is comfortable, casual dress (ties are out!) as you will be sitting on low, soft ottomans or lolling back on cushions.

Once at El Mansour, all you need do is choose your main dish because all other courses are set along standard Moroccan lines. You start with Harira, a spicy lentil-lamb soup which you drink directly from the bowl. Next comes the classic Moroccan salad of chopped tomatoes and green peppers surrounding chopped eggplant. This refreshing melange is aromatic with cumin, the ubiquitous spice of Morocco; and it is eaten with chunks of bread employed shovel-fashion. Then you are served the great "piece de resistance"—Bastela, a hot, paper-thin filo-dough pie encasing a mad mixture of chicken, eggs and nuts all scented with cinnamon and spices and sweetened with sugar. The taste is so addictive, you will find yourself risking singed fingers to eat it quickly. For a main course, I favor the unusually succulent Chicken with Lemon. Other people in your party may opt for any of the many lamb dishes, Lamb and Almonds being my preference; or for the excellent Couscous, a steaming plate of semolina topped with an assortment of vegetables and lamb. But to me, Moroccan dining is a communal experience so why not have everyone order a different main course and all share in, no holds barred! It may be messy, but it's great fun. Your fingers will become even stickier as you sample your dessert of a deep-fried, honey-glazed pastry. Sweet green mint tea—the finale to any meal or business deal in Morocco—completes your feast. Moderate prices.

10:00 p.m. Since you are in casual clothes whether you dined at El Mansour or Schroeder's, why not take in a disco? In fact, you can dance your ass off at Dance Your Ass Off, Inc., 901 Columbus at Lombard, any night of the week until 2:00 a.m. Buzzby's, 1436 Polk Street, is another popular discoteque with a predominantly gay clientele. There are many, many other discos in San Francisco but since the life expectancy of this type of enterprise is not too certain, listing the current ones here would be futile. The best place to get an up-to-the-minute reading on what is happening when and where in the entire Bay Area is in the Date Book Section of the *Sunday San Francisco Examiner & Chronicle,* the city's only Sunday newspaper. There you will find listings of all jazz joints, nightclubs, and music events.

Your 4th Perfect Day Schedule

9:30 a.m. A Spartan juice-and-coffee breakfast is what's recommended this morning before we embark on our tour through . . .

10:00 a.m. Chinatown! The largest in the Western world. I will take you on a personally conducted mini-tour, pointing out where to buy everything from jade to ginseng, from wicker to woks.

12:00 noon Your choice of a Chinatown lunch either at an authentic back-street noodle shop or at the granddaddy of Chinatown's luxury dining rooms.

2:00 p.m. Rest your feet while you give your eyes and ears a treat at either a performance of the symphony, opera, theater or even a good movie. Yes, I recommend a movie as an ideal sightseeing breather!

5:00 p.m. Wile away the cocktail hours from a downtown aerie from which you can watch the commuter traffic struggle home.

7:30 p.m. Fresh fish, fanciful French or just superb prime ribs of beef are the mainstay of the three restaurant recommendations for tonight.

10:00 p.m. Sprawl in front of your hotel TV to see if you can catch one of the San Francisco based shows—by now, you should know your way around better than the movie cameras! Tomorrow brings Japantown and Union Street.

The Fourth Day of Your
One Perfect Week in San Francisco

9:30 a.m. If you followed my disco-dancing directions last night, you should appreciate this slightly delayed opening of your fourth perfect day. Try to forgo breakfast or at least limit it to a Spartan juice-and-coffee because we have a very exciting Chinese lunch planned at noon. Should you wish to avoid the stratospheric prices of room service and your hotel does not boast a good coffee shop, you may wish to visit Manning's Cafeteria, 347 Geary Street, right off Union Square. It is the last of what was once a San Francisco tradition—good, well-run, comfortable cafeterias.

10:00 a.m. Because I will personally conduct you from shop to shop through San Francisco's world-famous Chinatown, it is best we begin at that quarter's official entrance— the ornate Chinese gate on the corner of Bush and Grant. If you are staying either on Nob Hill or in the Union Square area, it is only a short walk or cab ride. In fact, the reason our Chinatown is so popular for shopping and dining with localites as well as visitors is that it is centrally located, immediately adjacent to the downtown hub of the city. This, for example, is not the case in New York where you must undertake a lengthy subway or cab ride far from midtown Manhattan. So now it's off to Chinatown. Oh, yes, bring along those postcards you wrote yesterday. We will pass a post office where you can buy stamps at their face values, thus avoid being ripped off by those exorbitantly priced postage machines.

As we pass through the Chinatown gate, try not to notice those two hamburger eateries blighting the entrance on both sides. Instead, you might wish to hum the melody from "Flower Drum Song"—"Grant Avenue, San Francisco,

U.S.A."—for that is indeed the street on which we will be concentrating this morning. Let us start up the right-hand side.

Almost immediately we come upon our first stop: The City of Hankow Tassel Company, 406-420 Grant Avenue. The entrance at 420 takes you directly into the department for which this highly regarded store is most noted: excellent Chinese furniture and a marvelous collection of brass fittings —door knockers, drapery holders, cabinet fixtures, and every conceivable type of hardware. Chinese furnishings have always found a sizeable market in the Western world. And with today's trends toward clean, uncluttered lines, a handsomely designed Chinese table or chair, made of well-seasoned hardwood, can be a prized addition to almost any home—which is just the type of furnishings The City of Hankow Tassel Company excels in. You will also find a wide selection of lamps and lamp bases, as well as many decorative items, both antique and modern, from mainland China. Wearing apparel is featured in the section at 406 Grant; however, the furnishings are what have earned this shop its fine reputation.

Tai Chong, 506 Grant, has everything so look carefully. Amidst the "tourist trinkets," you will often find some very attractive items such as superior carved wooden corners for doorways, and small art objects. And among the gaudy satins, you might even discover some old silks which, today, are nearly unobtainable.

Gumling Importing Company, 544 Grant, is an attractive little shop with a commendable jewelry selection. (If you are considering serious jade purchases, wait for Wing Key later on.) Take a look at the ladies' oriental kimonos and small art objects.

Old St. Mary's Church, on the corner of Grant and California, dates from 1854. The original shell of brick, most of which was quarried in China and shipped in sailing vessels across the vast Pacific, withstood the quake which triggered the '06 fire, but the interior was totally gutted. Today, this charming church holds a special place in the affections of all San Franciscans. Opposite the church on California Street is St. Mary's Square, a pleasant sunning spot for financial-district lunchers, watched over by the late Benny Bufano's imposing statue of Sun Yat Sen.

The Canton Bazaar, 616 Grant, is a large Chinese emporium where the unpracticed eye can have difficulty separating the antiques from the mass-made, although the price tags might be considered clues. If you are making a serious purchase, you may wish to buy subject to an impartial appraisal, a worthwhile caution in any shop.

Lun On, 771 Sacramento just below Grant, is an old established specialist in bamboo and rattan. An ideal take-home purchase is a bamboo food protector for outdoor entertaining. It is easy to pack and makes a delightful gift.

Further down Sacramento Street at 755, you will find an unusual building housing the Nam Kue Elementary School. You might want to take a picture, especially to show the youngsters back home.

Now, back up to Grant Avenue where one block later, you will find Clay Street; a few doors downhill at 753 is a U.S. Post Office where you can mail those postcards. (They also accept parcel post, should you wish to ship some purchases home.)

Our first food shop on today's tour is Shing Chong at 800 Grant. This is one of Chinatown's oldest food emporiums and the range of its stock is marvelous. Be sure to note the large glass jars on the top shelf along the right-hand wall. They contain "thousand-year-eggs" and other Chinese delicacies. Incidentally, despite the eggs' colorful name, they are only a mere 90 days old!

The Wok Shop, 804 Grant, is a rather recent addition to the scene. Interest in Chinese cuisine has been growing by leaps and bounds. And a shop where Westerners could purchase the requisite cooking equipment was a natural. The Wok Shop carries a nice assortment of Chinese cookbooks and also packets of Chinese vegetable seeds for growing the ingredients back home. However, do check out the selection of culinary equipment at The Ginn Wall Company (a little later on in our tour) prior to making any purchases which interest you.

At the next street corner, Washington, walk downhill a few yards to number 743 to take a look at the marvelously colorful Bank of Canton building—for many years the special telephone exchange for Chinatown. Returning back up Washington Street, cross Grant and continue uphill. On the corner of Waverly Place and Washington, you will find The Dai Fook Company, 162 Waverly, a very large jewelry store with a tremendous array of jade.

However, the most crucial decision at this juncture is not which ring to buy, but rather where to lunch. I have two suggestions for today, both conveniently located in Chinatown, yet quite different from one another in style, ambience and cost.

Kan's is perhaps Chinatown's oldest de luxe Chinese restaurant. After World War II, it was Johnny Kan who first placed Chinese cuisine, prepared by master chefs, in elegant surroundings where it could be viewed and savored as an art form. Today, Kan's is still Chinatown's most famous restaurant and numbers among its regulars such chopstick fanatics as Danny Kaye. At Kan's you will be served beautifully prepared Cantonese dishes in spacious surroundings with menu prices in line with the quality and fine service.

On the other hand, The Golden Dragon Noodle Shop is a bustling, crowded, quick-order lunch spot which makes no concessions to Westerners. But it does dish up incredibly fine Chinese noodle dishes at prices that are positively bargain-basement. And since you are, at this moment, almost standing in front of The Golden Dragon Noodle Shop at 833 Washington (right across the alley from Dai Fook), it is a convenient time to make your luncheon choice, even though you may wish to wait a while. To aid you in your selection, you can watch the Noodle Shop's kitchen action through the sidewalk windows. Here you will see the chefs swiftly prepare each order of noodles or won ton, or cleave up orders of roast duck. And in case you think won tons are pedestrian, just look at how different these miniature beauties with their gossamer-thin skins are from most! They are the best in town. Should the sights through the window tempt you sufficiently, you will require more assistance when inside because most of the waiters speak little or no English and the menu translations tell you little. So let me help.

My favorite dish is Big Dumplings in Supreme Soup. In a bowl of homemade chicken stock float jumbo-sized dumplings, the nearly transparent casings holding a delicious filling of fresh shrimp and vegetables which veritably crunch beneath your bite. The cost of this superb dish is about $1.50! Of course, you may wish to try a bowl of those tiny won tons you saw in the window, or a combination bowl of won ton and some of those vermicelli-thin noodles. Those same won tons are also served with barbecued pork, and the noodles can be ordered with roasted duck. (However, please note that Chinese prefer their fowl and pork on the fatty side.) Aside from the noodles and won ton in soup, The Golden Dragon also serves Braised Noodles (or dry noodles) with a Hot Meat Sauce. And you've also got to have either Tender Greens or Chinese Broccoli in Oyster Sauce on the side—one portion for every 2 persons in your party. Cooked in under-done Chinese fashion, they positively burst with flavor and are the perfect accompaniment to the rich noodles. No matter what you decide upon, remember that this place is a noodle shop and that name is not used in vain. Don't expect American chop suey or sweet and sour pork. But do expect some of the greatest noodles and won ton outside Taiwan!

And for what to expect in Kan's, be sure to read ahead.

Now, having made your luncheon plans, our Chinatown tour must move along. So it's up Washington Street to take a peek into The Superior Trading Company, 837 Washington. This is a "modern" version of the famed old medicine and herb shops you may have read about. I say "modern" because the countless drawers with their mysterious treasures of roots, herbs and spices are conveniently labeled to help the clerk. In the ancient herb shops, the owners prided themselves on knowing the contents of each drawer and would have died of shame rather than label them. Only a little further on at 857 Washington, you will find Tai Fung Wo and Company which still operates in the time-honored, unlabeled style of old China.

And the style of old China and today's Chinese-American customs do indeed exist in our Chinatown side by side, as you can witness at 863 Washington, the Tong Hing Pastry Shop. Its claim to fame? Apple pie! Apple pie, that all-American dessert, is a great favorite among the Chinese community, exceeded perhaps only by coconut-custard pies and sponge cakes covered with whipped cream. Chances are you will see all three in this popular shop.

Continuing further up Washington Street, you will come to Stockton Street—turn right. Many years ago, Stockton Street was technically outside the strict confines of China-town proper. However, with the ever-increasing influx of visitors to Chinatown, the demand for shops selling "tourist trinkets" like back scratchers and such, began to push the non-tourist oriented shops from Grant Avenue. And the food stores were the first to go, regrouping on a few blocks of Stockton Street where the aromas of their products have made this street more authentically Chinese than parts of Grant Avenue.

Not only have the food stores found haven on Stockton Street but other firms who deal primarily with Chinese clientele have also relocated here. And perhaps the most important is the Wing Key Jewelry, 1028 Stockton. Wing Key is one of the most highly respected purveyors of ex-quisite jade. As with everything else these days, jade is not inexpensive. (By the way, Wing Key has an even larger branch on the corner of Grant and Maiden Lane in the Livingston's store.)

Now, by crossing Stockton Street to the odd-numbered side, you can throw yourself into the throngs of Chinese women as they stock up on fresh produce, fish and poultry. With the reliance of Chinese cooking on the ultimate in fresh ingredients, daily shopping is a necessity. And the examination some of these women put each vegetable or wall-eyed fish through, is remarkable to behold.

Two blocks along Stockton Street, you will reach Pacific Avenue. Turn right (downhill) here, and return to Grant Avenue where another right turn heads you back downtown. This time you can take in the shops on the odd-numbered side, crossing over to number 1016, The Ginn Wall Company, to investigate their collection of woks and Chinese culinary equipment.

Back across the street at 903, you will find Fat Ming Company, a Chinese stationery shop with a marvelous array of greeting cards from Hong Kong. Decorated with traditional Chinese artwork and characters, but with English messages, they make novel and beautiful greetings.

Two blocks further on, you will find yourself opposite Kan's, 708 Grant Avenue, (982-2388). One of the greatest joys of a Cantonese lunch is its diversity yet lightness. From Kan's special luncheon menu, you can relish a wide spectrum of flavors and textures without having your afternoon activities inhibited by any feeling of heaviness. For example, I would suggest you begin with their excellent So See Chicken, a Chinese salad of shredded lettuce, chicken, coriander and some ground nuts for texture. Then, since it is customary to eschew rice at lunch in favor of noodles, be sure to order Pan Fried Noodles with Tomato Beef, one of my favorites at Kan's. Here, little beef filets are delicately tender, the tomatoes refreshingly sweet and the noodles possessing just a hint of crispness.

As in any Chinese meal, except perhaps "dim sum," vegetables are a must. One of Kan's most popular dishes is Asparagus Beef; but naturally, it is only available during spring when that king of vegetables is in season. However, always inquire of your waiter or maitre d' which vegetables are on hand. During the summer, you will usually find broccoli or long beans (those yard-long, whip-like beans which you may have spotted earlier in a market). Either one makes a handsome accompaniment to beef or pork. Oh, yes, request that the beans or broccoli be minced. To end your lunch on a mellow note, order an Almond Eye, a satiny-smooth drink invented at Kan's.

And if you are as impressed with Kan's luncheon culinary achievements as hundreds of thousands of other diners are each year, you might ask to see a dinner menu. There, you will discover a wealth of classics, such as Kan's own inimitable version of Peking Duck, Lemon Chicken, and Winter Melon Soup. If you are tempted into a return visit for dinner later in your stay, be certain you check in advance whether any of the dishes which intrigue you need be ordered in advance. Moderate prices.

We have two remaining stops of interest on our tour. The first is at 527 Grant, The House of Sung. This is probably Chinatown's finest antique dealer with a collection of museum-quality pieces. You are most welcome to inspect their treasures. However, I would admonish you not to take any young children into the shop. A slight mishap could cost you thousands!

Our last stop is on the same side of Grant Avenue at 437, where you will discover a shop called Filia which features an incredible array of beads, both strung and loose. Among them are ivory, jade and many semi-precious ones, along with the inevitable glass. And now you are only a few steps from our point of origin as well as the end of our Chinatown tour—the dragon gate.

2:00 p.m. After a morning on your feet, I have planned a "sit-down" afternoon. And that means either a play, musical, symphony, opera or movie—all depending on what day of the week it is, as well as what time of year.

If today is almost any Thursday from early December to early June, you might wish to attend an afternoon performance of the famed San Francisco Symphony. For decades, the matinee audience has consisted predominantly of women who have made these performances a social habit. Their custom of wearing "correct" gloves once prompted Papa Pierre Monteux, the late-great former symphony conductor, to remark that he could hardly hear the ladies' applause!

The Thursday afternoon concerts seldom sell out, so you should have little difficulty obtaining tickets right at the Opera House, located in the Civic Center at Van Ness and Grove Street. It might be advisable, though, to plan ahead and purchase your seats at the Symphony Box Office (421-1000) located in the Sherman Clay Music Store, on Kearny Street between Post and Sutter. (You pay no additional charge for any tickets obtained from this official symphony box office. Tickets bearing a service charge can often be purchased from the various ticket agencies throughout the downtown area and in many hotel lobbies.)

If your musical interests lie toward the lyric theater, consider yourself extremely fortunate if today's date reads anywhere from mid-September to December 1, and it is a Saturday or Sunday. For those two and a half months, it's opera time in San Francisco and one of the greatest opera companies in the world holds the Opera House stage. You most likely can uncover a ticket to the Saturday matinee, but you may have to search a bit to uncover one to the usually standing-room-only Sunday matinee. Whatever tickets are available can be obtained at the opera box office in the Opera House lobby (431-1210). If they are sold out, you might try one of the independent ticket agencies. Failing this, you can try to unearth a turn-in at the last minute. However, on a sure-fire sellout such as a Joan Sutherland performance, ticket seekers surround the opera house pleading with arriving patrons for that chance extra ducat which would allow them entry.

Once inside, the Opera House itself is something to see. While it does not possess the elaborate red damask aura of old-fashioned European houses, it is happily not the cold, unfinished concrete and exposed steel of its contemporary sisters. It has spaciousness, comfort, and especially in the upper reaches, fine acoustics. Also, unlike many older theaters, the sight lines are excellent with only a small section of the orchestra seats down front on the extreme sides not having a total view of the stage. (As I mentioned on our first perfect day out, the Opera House is a twin structure to the Veterans' Building, across the carriage entrance and garden. Both it and the Opera House served as the site of the signing of the United Nations Charter in April 1945.)

From spring through mid-fall, the Civic Light Opera holds its season of musicals. Four different productions are usually mounted for several weeks each. They range from exact imports or duplications of Broadway's best to classic revivals and even operettas. Ticket availability is solely dependent upon the success of the particular offering. If you see an ad in the daily newspaper for the current production, then you will have little trouble locating tickets. If not, you still might try one of the regular ticket agencies.

San Francisco has always had a strong theatrical tradition dating back to the '49er days. In fact, the thundering of the miners' heavy boots on the bare wooden floors literally could "bring down the house"! Post-World War II days found touring companies and a host of small repertory companies (the most famous being the Actor's Workshop) filling the playbills. Today, the old-time Broadway touring companies which once were the domain of Katherine Cornell, Eva Le Gallienne, Tallulah, and others have all but disappeared. And as the good dramatists dwindled, so too the "little theaters." Besides, the few remaining "little theaters" seldom stage matinees.

Today's theater tradition in San Francisco has been kept alive and thriving by the city's American Conservatory Theater. With a season that takes over the Geary Theater stage (occasionally overflowing to the stage of the smaller Marines' Memorial Theater, too) from early fall to early summer, the A.C.T. fills theatrical appetites with a steady diet of classics, revivals, contemporary and avant garde offerings, often presented in a highly original and, at times, controversial style. The dominance of local legitimate theater by the A.C.T. has also put them in the position of sponsoring what few touring companies there are, which has included England's Old Vic.

Tickets for the A.C.T. are available at the Geary Theater (673-6440), one and a half blocks off Union Square, as well as at most ticket agencies. So between the A.C.T. and the Civic Light Opera, nearly every Wednesday and Saturday is matinee day in San Francisco.

Many people think that going to a movie is a waste of time while on vacation or on a visit to a new city. I disagree. I think that any full week of strictly sightseeing can become tiring if one doesn't stop once in a while to relax and refuel. And for me, there is no better place to lose myself than in the escape of a darkened movie house where I can become totally occupied by the images on the screen. And if you find a film you have not seen, you might also discover that viewing it at a matinee is not only a pleasant change of pace but a bargain as well, since many cinemas offer reduced prices before 5:00 p.m.

If there are no theatrical offerings to interest you this afternoon, you might take a very leisurely stroll through one of our museums, again not trying to see everything in all the galleries but just settling down in front of a few favorites in peace and quiet.

5:00 p.m. Having spent your afternoon in a darkened theater, a refreshing contrast might be cocktails from a different vantage point of the city. For this, I recommend the Starlite Roof of the Hotel Sir Francis Drake, conveniently located at Powell and Sutter Streets. This unusually spacious room presents a truly magnificent view of the Bay Area. From its southern and eastern windows, you get a bird's-eye view of the five o'clock commuter-crammed freeways and Bay Bridge approach. You can indeed feel smug as you settle back with no traffic tie-ups to bedevil you and with nothing more critical to contemplate than where to dine this evening. Here are three recommendations to consider.

7:30 p.m. The House of Prime Rib, 1906 Van Ness at Washington, (885-4605), is the restaurant for people who cannot make up their minds about what to order. You see, at the House of Prime Rib, there is no choice—only prime ribs of beef. Oh, there are minor variations as to size of cut and degree of doneness, but that's the extent of it. So if you are in a roast beef mood, then the House of Prime Rib is an excellent choice. A delicious green salad enhanced by julienne beets and chopped egg, flavored with the special celery-seed accented house dressing, is the perennial opener. Then from their trolley, you select the size cut of roast beef you wish, specifying rare, medium rare or (perish the thought) well done. The quality of their beef is among the best in town and less costly than most comparable versions. Yorkshire pudding, mashed potatoes and creamed spinach are the invariable accompaniments. At extra charge, you can opt for an enormous baked potato in lieu of the mashed (two persons can easily share one order). Desserts are on the simple side: superb Pecan Pie, fresh pineapple and fresh strawberries in season. Aside from savoring the excellent quality food, handsomely prepared, you also will be able to witness the "performance" of a team of waitresses which sets bench marks for efficiency and courtesy. Moderate prices.

Fleur de Lys, 777 Sutter Street near Jones, (673-7779), is one of the city's most dramatically beautiful restaurants. Seemingly acres of tropical floral print have converted the room into an Arabian Nights pleasure tent with mirrored side panels reflecting the patrons into infinity. However, this dazzling decor in no way overshadows the cuisine which numbers among its selections some of my favorite dishes. The Herring in White Wine, for example, cannot be faulted for either its quality or its delicious creamy wine sauce. Another excellent cold first course is a vichyssoise-like watercress soup, while the house pate, correctly served with those tart little cornichons, is equally winning. My ultimate first course does not appear on the menu and is available only in the fall. Should you be here then, be certain to inquire of your maitre d' if there are any fresh mussels on hand. Lamb is one of the great meats of the West and Fleur de Lys does itself proud with two fine presentations: a tantalizingly pink rack of lamb served with a snappy ratatouille (that Provencale melange of peppers, eggplant, tomatoes and garlic) and a lamb filet roasted "en Chemise" (in a flaky pastry crust). Since I have warned you away from veal in all but the finest restaurants, now is your chance to enjoy this delicate meat in a Piccata de Veau aux Courgettes. Here, the finest of veal alternates with slices of fresh zucchini, all lightly bathed in a lemon-butter sauce.

Desserts, once the Achilles heel of this kitchen, have been upgraded to stellar status. My favorite is the Profiteroles. Three little homemade cream puff shells are filled with ice cream—but not in advance!—and treated to a dark chocolate sauce. Also, some fresh fruit or berry tarts are hiding somewhere just waiting for your fork to crush their tender flake pastry. Not that expensive when you consider the stunning decor, careful service and delicious cuisine.

Tadich Grill, 240 California Street near Front, (391-2373), is one of San Francisco's oldest restaurants dating from 1849. It is also one of the very few fine seafood restaurants in our city-by-the-bay (strange as it may seem), which easily accounts for its enormous popularity. Therefore, if you decide upon dining at Tadich's, you can depend on two things for sure—a long, long wait (no reservations are accepted) and the finest in fresh seafood. Happily, the latter more than compensates for the former. In fact, the mass of imbibing patrons packed around the small bar usually develops a camaraderie which is positively infectious. Once I am seated, however, I don't have to wait another minute since I know just what I will have—and invariably, it's one of Tadich's fresh fish selections. My choice is naturally dependent upon what is "in season."

Always available are the fresh water baby salmon, those delicately pink little beauties now commercially bred. During the summer, the regular sea salmon is exceptionally fine here as is the petrale, a local variety of flatfish. Fresh sea bass is another sure-fire selection. Because these fish are large and flavorful enough to take the slight searing of hot coals, I request they be charcoal broiled. The fragile little sand dabs, usually between seven and nine inches, require the gentler ministrations of frying to preserve their haunting sweetness. And just watch the stellar job the waiter does in boning them! Abalone, that marvelous mollusk of the California seacoast, is another Tadich star. And here, they treat the delicately subtle, almost baby veal-like flesh to the proper handling with just a light dusting of cracker crumbs.

Should you have a non-seafood fancier in your party, do not despair. The skirt steak, a good old-fashioned flank steak, is extraordinarily juicy and tasty. For starters, the shrimp cocktail is impeccable (made of the tiny "baby" shrimp) and the Boston clam chowder is worthwhile. For dessert, the rice custard pudding is a nostalgic relic of the restaurant's 19th-century dining style, while the fresh melon in season is always of prime quality. But a word of caution: at precisely 8:30 p.m. by the old-time schoolhouse clock on the wall, the shades are drawn and the front door locked. It would be far easier for a camel to pass through the eye of a needle than for another patron to crowd into Tadich's after that hour. Moderate prices, considering it is San Francisco's ultimate seafood house.

10:00 p.m.   Again, it has been a long day . . . with even more walking planned for tomorrow. So my suggestion now is to head back to your hotel, sprawl out on your bed and perhaps catch a rerun of "Streets of San Francisco" or "Ironside" or any of the dozens of films which have used this most photogenic of all American cities as the backdrop. And since you are such a San Francisco hand by now, try and spot the geographic errors, such as having a police chase begin at the Golden Gate Bridge Plaza and end two seconds later atop Potrero Hill. Now, you and I both know that's not quite possible. Right? Pleasant dreams.

Your 5th Perfect Day Schedule

9:00 a.m.   Breakfast at a kosher-style deli, the Stage.

10:00 a.m.   A walking tour of Japantown, where yesterday and tomorrow meet in the flutter of cherry blossoms along a peaceful mall, and in the glare and blare of electronics equipment in a modern trade center.

12:00 noon   Lunch at an authentic Japanese restaurant where both novice and Nipponphile can savor the finest tempura and gyoza in town.

1:45 p.m.   A journey through San Francisco's past, strolling down the tree-shaded streets of famed Pacific Heights, one of the poshest urban neighborhoods in America.

3:00 p.m.   Union Street—part Carnaby Street, part carnival—is today's shops housed on a yesterday street. Late afternoon cocktails in one of its famed "watering spots," or a wine-and-cheese tasting.

5:00 p.m.   Head back to your hotel for a well-earned rest.

8:30 p.m.   Dine on de luxe French cuisine or enjoy the finest in creative American cooking with a flair.

10:30 p.m.   I don't know about you, but I am bushed!

The Fifth Day of Your
One Perfect Week in San Francisco

9:00 a.m. Today will be your chance to experience more of the feel of this marvelous city—through the soles of your feet! It will be a day that can be savored only by a good deal of walking—ambling down a stone-paved Japanese mall, strolling through the quiet tree-shaded streets of luxurious Pacific Heights, browsing in and out of the crazy-quilt warren of shops along Union Street. In all, today will be a kaleidoscope of sights, uniquely San Francisco.

Of all the itineraries in this book, today's was the most difficult to map out. In leading you from one area to another, I wanted to avoid any strenuous climbs—a near-impossible feat in hilly San Francisco. But by following my directions, you can effortlessly take the day in stride. There will be no need for a car, for we will travel by foot and public transportation. Be sure you have a good supply of quarters, as the city's bus drivers do not make change. Now then, two prerequisites are essential: a good pair of walking shoes and a full-sized breakfast. You supply the former and I will take care of the latter by suggesting the Stage Delicatessen, 424 Geary Street near Mason, (776-8968).

The single block of Geary, bound by Mason and Taylor Streets, for years has been regarded as San Francisco's "Theater District" because standing on the south side are the Curran and Geary Theaters, the town's principal legitimate theaters. And just as on New York's Broadway where bagels go with lox and pastrami seems congenial to Pirandello, the north side of Geary boasts not one, not two, but three kosher-style delicatessens! David's was the first on the block. No doubt it was his enormous success which soon lured Solomon to move in. Then, almost as a buffer zone between the two biblical kings, the Stage Delicatessen was established. Perhaps because it demonstrates the "we're not first so we try harder" philosophy, my personal favorite at the moment is the Johnny-come-lately Stage Deli.

Since it is open from early morning to past midnight, you can sample the Stage's kosher-style cooking during any hour of the day. Today, however, we are concerned with breakfast, which is a fine time to partake of that great Jewish classic: Nova Scotia salmon (lox) and cream cheese on a bagel. This combination of freshly sliced smoked salmon, creamy cheese, topped with sweet Bermuda onion rings, all on a delicately bland bagel, is the staple of almost every Jewish Sunday breakfast-brunch. It might be considered an acquired taste, but once acquired it is addictive! Another Jewish breakfast favorite and one that the Stage does extremely well is a tasty blend of smoked salmon and onions mixed into scrambled eggs. Of course, you can enjoy eggs in almost any style, served with bacon or knockwurst. And while there is nothing Jewish about French toast, at the Stage it rises above the mundane when made from challah egg bread, soaked in fresh egg and beautifully grilled. The sweet breakfast rolls (known in San Francisco by names such as snails and bear claws) are made on the premises, and they are excellent. In true San Francisco tradition, however, the coffee is just passable.

10:00 a.m. With the last morsel of raisin snail cleaned from your plate, it is time to head out. Exit from the Stage to your left. You need walk only a few feet to the bus stop where you will board a #38 bus. Ask the driver to call out Webster Street; if he remembers, your destination should be called in about ten minutes. On leaving the bus, cross Webster Street (note the street sign is also written in Japanese characters), turn right, and enter the doors at 1581 Webster, directly adjacent to a Crocker Bank.

In the 1950's, when Japanese trade with the United States began to burgeon and tourism across the Pacific took on the aspects of a commute run, Japanese business interests drew up plans for a culture-and-trade center that would not only showcase Japanese products, but cement stronger cultural ties with San Francisco. Discussions, plans and the inevitable delays seemed to go on without end. Finally, the three-block long complex, which you have just entered, materialized. Whether the idea was too grandiose or the site, appropriately located in San Francisco's "Japantown," was too distant from downtown shopping and foot traffic, the success the planners envisioned has never been achieved. For example, the enormous Kabuki Theater, which was launched with glittering imported Japanese reviews, bit the dust shortly after opening. And while the Miyako Hotel, which towers over the east end of the center, enjoys capacity business, the trade center itself does not seem to attract too much interest. I suspect the lack of great success can be attributed also to the center's obvious touristy air, with bazaar-style shops and such come-on's as "pearls in every oyster" attractions. Nevertheless, the center is well worth a brief walk-through and you can start by climbing the stairs directly in front of you.

On reaching the upper level, proceed across the covered bridge which usually contains some fine examples of Japanese art on loan from the Avery Brundage Collection, housed in Golden Gate Park. Directly before you on the east side of the bridge you will find one of my favorite stops in the center, the Ikenobo Ikebana Society Headquarters. Ikebana is the art of arranging flowers. And here, in the showcase windows, you can feast your eyes on a few outstanding examples. Practitioners of this delicate art form can achieve more grace and beauty with one iris, a single leaf and a bent twig, than I have ever seen anybody do with two dozen long stem roses! If you are interested in learning more about the age-old art and traditions of ikebana, here is your opportunity.

Only a few doors away from the serene, frozen poetry of ikebana, you will come in contact with the jazzy, garish glitter of the dozens of Japanese TV sets currently on the market. However, another feast for the eye, if not for the pocketbook, is the Murata Pearls displayed right across the way. At the end of the long arcade is the official Japan Information Service, run by the Consulate General of Japan. If you contemplate ever journeying to the fabled city of Kyoto, here is where you should stop to garner all the information you will need.

Immediately on passing the information center, you will exit from the west wing of the center onto the Peace Plaza, with the Peace Pagoda rising above its reflecting pool. Here you might wish to sit a moment and look out over the western half of the city. There is little need to bother with the east wing of the center since it only houses less of the same.

Directly across Post Street from the Peace Plaza is the latest addition to Japantown, one that I believe represents a more beautiful way to attract visitors to the area. For unlike the huge concrete dinosaur of the center, the shopping mall you see before you is far more evocative of what most Westerners like to think of as Japan. True, the center is more representative of today's concrete-and-steel Tokyo. But we have enough concrete and steel in our own cities, and travelers search for something else.

In 1907, when the Japanese colony resettled here in the "Western Addition" after the '06 fire, the buildings had no oriental flair. Unlike Chinatown, which was devastated in the fire and rebuilt with nods to Chinese architectural styles, Japantown consisted of Victorian wood houses dating from the late 19th century. The fire never reached this area; by dynamiting Van Ness Avenue, it was confined to what we know as the downtown area and Nob Hill. When these old wood buildings began to deteriorate beyond repair, nondescript, more modern dwellings and shops replaced them. Then, a few years ago, instead of waiting for the old structures on this block of Buchanan Street to tumble one by one, they were razed and a Japanese village street of yesteryear rose in their place. Down the center of the wide mall curves a serpentine pattern of stones, connecting two foun-

tains made of stone and iron. The cherry blossom trees and
azaleas bloom in the spring and if you are here at that time
of year, you can watch their blossoms flutter earthward as
you sit on one of the benches. The shops bordering the mall
sell today's Japanese electronic products and the like, but
they also contain some of the finest examples of folk art
and kimonos. It is a lovely place to enjoy a sunny San Francisco day.

Before you take in the mall, however, cross Post Street
and turn right along the street's north side. There are a
couple of shops you might enjoy browsing through. For example, on the corner is Soko Hardware. Never will you see
such a clutter of wares, including all manner of supplies,
pots and planters for bonsai growers. Further down the
street at number 1656 Post is the Uoki Sakai Company. In
this grocery store, you can view the finest and freshest of
vegetables arranged by hands which must have been trained
in ikebana! And if you think you have sampled just about
every known product of our earth, just glance through the
displays of gobo, daikon and other roots and greens, all part
of Japanese gardening and cuisine.

Now, retrace your steps to the mall. As you amble up
the slight incline, you may wish to check the dates on the
posters announcing festivals in the community. If one is
happening during your stay, a return visit might be in order
to witness some time-honored traditions. Continue your walk
to Honnami Taieido, 1722 Buchanan. In this lovely shop,
you will find some of the finest examples of modern Japanese
folk art. You can revel in the incredible beauty of pottery
by Shoji Hamada, acknowledged as the master craftsman
of today. You may also notice some very remarkable pottery
by another Hamada, Shoji Hamada's second son, who has
not yet achieved his father's artistry—or price. A few doors
further up at 1758 Buchanan is Sanko, a treasure trove of
modern Japanese wares—sake sets, rice bowls, etc., which
make lovely gifts.

When you reach the top of the mall, cross Sutter Street
to the American Fish Market. Since one of the glories of

Japanese cuisine is sashimi (raw fish), the freshness of sea products is of infinite importance. And the American Fish Company carries a wide variety of tuna, favored for sashimi, as well as octopus and other denizens of the deep. In the far left corner is a tiny sushi counter, where cold rice and seaweed are used as the major ingredients to create a style of snack food, uniquely Japanese. Definitely an acquired taste!

On leaving the American Fish Company, be sure to take a look at the two buildings almost directly across Sutter Street (Nos. 1771-1777 and 1783-1787). Both were constructed in the 1880's as "double houses" with each house later turned into a duplex. They are fine examples of Victorian San Francisco architecture of slightly different styles. The lower numbered building is in the "Italianate style," while its neighbor is in the "Stick style." At a glance, they may appear to be identical, but closer observation will uncover a wealth of variations in the details which make them really quite dissimilar. (For readers with more than a cursory interest in architecture, I heartily recommend: *Here Today: San Francisco's Architectural Heritage,* sponsored by the Junior League of San Francisco, Inc. and published by Chronicle Books.)

Now, walk back down the right-hand side of the mall, browsing through some of the shops there, such as the N.B. Kimono Store. At the bottom of the mall, turn right a few feet and you will find yourself at one of the finest Japanese restaurants in San Francisco. Since it is open for lunch—which is what you should be considering about now—just walk right in.

12:00 noon When you enter Sanppo, 1702 Post Street, (346-3486), you could be entering any one of a thousand small restaurants in Japan. To say the place is clean is slanderous—it is immaculate. The sandal-shod waitresses dart in and around each other as though performing a ballet choreographed for swallows. And the cooking is superb, especially the tempura which is peerless in town. To the uninitiated, tempura is but one style of Japanese cooking, one in which a whole range of seafoods and vegetables can be covered with a light batter and then quickly deep-fried. It sounds simple enough but to insure the correct gossamer lightness and to avoid any signs of greasiness, a chef must have a built-in stopwatch. You will discover Sanppo's excellent tempura for yourself when a plate of shrimp, sweet potato slices and other fresh vegetables, all encased in their light batter-cocoons, are placed before you.

In fact, you might wish to split an order of tempura as a first course and then proceed to other dishes, such as the gyoza. Almost every ethnic variety of cooking has some manner of meat in pastry—Italy has its ravioli, Russia its pelmeni, China its kuo tieh, and Japan its gyoza. Gyoza is ground pork touched with garlic, enveloped in a paper-thin dough, and fried on one side only. Delicious! In salmon season, do not miss the magic a great Japanese chef can perform on this often maligned fish. And speaking of fish, Sanppo is an ideal place for the adventuresome to try the sashimi (raw fish). Of course, if you are fully acquainted with this great delicacy, you will appreciate Sanppo's masterful presentation, a delight to both eye and palate. Sanppo is an ideal restaurant for both the newcomer to Japanese cuisine as well as the Nipponphile, at moderate prices.

1:00 p.m. When you leave Sanppo, turn right and walk one and a half blocks to Fillmore Street. As you near Fillmore, it is a good time for me to point out another attraction of the Trade Center across the street which is traditionally Japanese, but of which you canot avail yourself right this moment—a shiatsu massage. Located in the far west end of the center is Kabuki Hot Spring (922-6000), a Japanese massage center. Here you can bask in the tension-releasing euphoria of a hot tub and sauna, followed by the shiatsu massage. This method concentrates on pressure points in the body rather than on the overall body-caressing usually associated with American or European massages. And you will find no hanky-panky at Kabuki—try the downtown area for that!

At Fillmore Street, turn left to the nearest bus stop, on the Geary Street overpass. Use another of your quarters to board a #22 bus, asking the driver to announce Jackson Street. Actually, it would be great fun to walk these nine blocks, but it probably would take its toll on your energies which you will need for later on. So sit back and relax while you observe the incredible cultural mix along the sidewalk—for on this section of Fillmore Street no one ethnic group has proprietary rights. You will see Japanese restaurants (the last outposts of Japantown), soul-food kitchens (the furthest extensions of lower Fillmore's black ghetto), Chinese lunch counters, antique-junk dealers, recycled clothes shops, etc. However, by the time your bus reaches Jackson Street, the neighborhood suddenly becomes less commercial —for you are on the threshold of Pacific Heights, one of the poshest urban neighborhoods in America.

1:45 p.m. Leave the bus at Jackson Street and walk one short block further to Pacific Avenue. Turn left on Pacific and you find yourself on a tree-shaded street, light-years removed from the atmosphere of only a few short blocks away. Here, the residential architecture varies greatly in style from the Classical Revival beauties at numbers 2418 and 2420 to the false-fronted Italianate of the Leale House at number 2475. Queen Anne, Baroque, and English are all to be seen. But more than lessons in architecture, these grand homes represent the wealth and taste of the founding families of San Francisco who built most of them in the closing years of the last century, high on these heights commanding a view of the entrance to the Bay, just as feudal lords built their castles on equally strategic points along the Rhine and Danube. You can share this eagle's-nest view by glancing down Steiner Street to the Bay and the hills beyond.

Five blocks along Pacific, turn right down Broderick Street to Broadway. Yes, this is the same street which houses the roaring, neon-bedecked topless joints of North Beach.

But the loudest sounds you may hear in this part of town probably will belong to the electric clocks of the silent Rolls-Royces as they glide by. Some of the most grandiose houses in San Francisco will be found on the next two blocks, to your left. For example, just look at the one at 2901! One block beyond, Broadway ends at a gate to the Presidio. So here, turn right and walk down the stairs alongside the Presidio fence to Vallejo, one block below.

I can never descend this flight of stairs without being taken back in time to a more leisurely era when these houses were constructed, when nannies sunned their charges on the park-like landings, when the domed Palace of Fine Arts you see before you was just one building in a fairy-tale city. Now, empty aluminum cans shock the greenery, blinded lamp posts cry for the public's disregard for civic beauty, and the great-great-grandchildren of the builders of these homes hurl expletives at passing drivers who dare force them to swerve their skateboards off course. At Vallejo Street, turn right and continue two blocks to Broderick; then downhill two blocks to Union Street.

3:00 p.m. At this point, you have a decision to make. If you feel that the pre-lunch walk combined with the one-hour tour through Pacific Heights have proven too much for your stamina, you can simply board a #41 bus and ride back to Union Square downtown, within a block of where your day began. Or, if you are still game—and I hope you are—you can turn right and proceed along Union Street, up the slight rise and over the top into what is the Carnaby Street of San Francisco.

Years ago, Union Street was a rather sedate shopping area, filled mostly with little antique stores run by quiet-spoken, gentlefolk. Then, some "with-it" boutiques began intermingling with the antiques. In their wake came the singles bars, the "watering spots" which cater to the young swingers in search of each other. So today, this six-block stretch of Union is a wild smattering of everything—fun and funky, garish and glamorous, sedate and insane. And you can pick and chose as your tastes dictate.

However, before your senses are assailed by all this, you might wish a calm moment to rest your feet by passing through the lych gate into the courtyard of St. Mary the Virgin's Episcopal Church at the corner of Union and Steiner. In this oasis, the silence is broken only by the splashing of waters from an artesian well into a fountain basin.

Now, on to Union Street. I will not provide you with a door-to-door guide for two reasons. First of all, the shops seem to have an unpredictable life span; and secondly, the range of tastes along this thoroughfare is so vast that it would be hopeless to cover the entire spectrum. So I will just point out a few I particularly enjoy. The first is at 2266 Union, the Toyoh. Here you will find oriental art objects of museum quality, with prices to match. On the same block at number 2224 is the Artist's Cooperative Gallery which showcases the art of some of the Bay Area's best.

On the corner of Fillmore and Union, you should take a short side trip down Fillmore to visit some especially outstanding shops. Mark Harrington, 3053 Fillmore, features the finest in crystal and all manner of stemware. Almost next door at number 3063 is Elaine Magnin's, a mecca for the needlework addict. And in the next block at number 3131 is one of the city's most respected oriental art shops, T. Z. Shiota. Heading back up to Union Street on the even-numbered side, you come across the Cultural Revolution, 3044 Fillmore, one of the first shops in the city and the nation to feature imports from mainland China. The shop, now under new management, will undergo a revolution all its own as it starts to bring the best of all varieties of folk arts and crafts to Fillmore Street. At number 3028 is Shibata's, another excellent oriental art dealer.

Back up at Union Street, turn left and you are in front of Jurgensen's at number 2190, one of the city's top grocers and fine-food emporiums. Here, the knowledgeable staff will gladly create handsome—let alone toothsome—baskets of fresh or preserved edibles which make ideal hostess or "thank-you" gifts.

Before I leave you to browse on your own, I'd like to give you a few more tips. First of all, don't keep your eyes riveted only to Union Street's tempting shop windows. Look up at the buildings themselves. While the displays may be of the latest hair styles or haute couturier fashions, the buildings, such as number 1980, are charming old relics, many dating from the late 1800's. Secondly, there are many little courtyards along Union which have nests of shops so keep an eye out for these, such as the one at number 2147. Also keep in mind that whenever you tire, you can always catch the #41 bus (heading east), which will carry you directly back downtown. And the last thing I want to mention is one of the most unusual houses in San Francisco, the Octagon House. Located right off Union at 2645 Gough (five blocks from Fillmore), this eight-sided structure dates from 1861 and its unusual shape was due to the then popular belief that the octagon represented good luck. It now houses a museum and is owned by the National Society of Colonial Dames.

Naturally, if thirst overcomes you along your Union sojourn, you can easily stop in at one of the numerous "watering holes" such as the popular Perry's at number 1944, or Thomas Lord's at number 2000. Or, if you are a lover of superb cheeses and fine wines, you may wish to drop by the Wine and Cheese Center at 2111 Union (563-3606). Here you can order almost any cheese your tastebuds desire, and wine—either a bottle in stock at retail shelf price or single glasses from the selections they have open for tasting on that day. If you opt for the glasses of wine, you can comparison sip while nibbling on a lovely cheese, fine pate, French bread and fruit. The Wine and Cheese Center is Union Street's answer to "a loaf of bread, a jug of wine, and ————" . . . (you fill in the blank).

5:00 p.m. Well, if you have not started back to your hotel, you had better. It has been a long day and you will want to rest before dinner.

8:30 p.m. For this evening, I have chosen two excellent restaurants which are very different from one another in style of cuisine and price.

L'Orangerie, 419 O'Farrell Street, (776-3600; reservations imperative). L'Orangerie today is regarded as one of San Francisco's greatest French restaurants. And the esteem in which it is held can be attributed to three extremely talented people: a superb chef, whose hallmark is refinement par excellence; an owner, who will tolerate no compromise of quality; and the city's most famous maitre d'hotel, Hans Brandt, who works magic with the dining room staff. Together, this formidable triumvirate can conjure up a never-to-be-forgotten dining experience.

For a first course, Oeufs Farcis Chimay is a devastatingly rich marriage of eggs, mushrooms and bechamel sauce. For something on the lighter side, the Quiche Lorraine is delicious and the smoked salmon gives testimony to the uncompromising standards of the owner. Or, if you wish to dine in a more de luxe French fashion, ask to split an order of English sole or turbot with someone else in your party. The exquisite delicacy of the flown-in English sole is beautifully retained by just a dusting of flour prior to its being gently sauteed in butter; the turbot is poached and served with a hauntingly lemony hollandaise sauce.

For a main course, I must confess prejudice toward the Carre de Porc a L'Orangerie. This succulent loin of pork is carved at tableside and then lightly bathed in a heavenly orange-cognac sauce. It has been my undying favorite since L'Orangerie first opened its doors. If you prefer a less complicated but equally superb dish, try the Poulet Roti Cressonniere. Roasting a chicken to perfection easily can be the acid test of any chef. And L'Orangerie's passes with flying golden colors on the crisped skin that harbors beneath it moistly tender flesh. For dessert, any lover of French cuisine will melt into ecstacy as the first taste of one of L'Orangerie's souffles melts in his or her mouth! And when you surround this refined style of French cuisine with sparkling table settings, a distinguished wine list, and impeccable service, you have the quintessence of fine San Francisco dining. As a grand finale, the warm library-bar provides a rosy setting for an after-dinner cognac in an atmosphere evocative of the mansions you viewed this afternoon. As with anything today, premium prices for premium quality.

Golden Eagle, 160 California at Front Street, (982-8831). Although the style of cuisine, the elaborateness of service and the range of prices at the Golden Eagle are unlike that of L'Orangerie, I regard this excellent restaurant with equal respect. And so do legions of San Franciscans who jam it to the bursting point at lunch. Because it is not in the heart of the downtown area, at night the dining room is less hectic; yet, the kitchen's output is no less rewarding. The Golden Eagle is what I call a "personal statement" restaurant, reflecting the tastes and culinary beliefs of the owners rather than their doggedly following any set theme. And since the cooking bears no particular ethnic stamp, it must be regarded as American—with a flair!

The soups at the Golden Eagle are especially inspired, making the full dinners irresistible. For a main course, I favor their Beef Vinaigrette not only because it is seldom encountered in restaurants today, but also because it is so superbly prepared here. Chicken Divine is probably the Golden Eagle's most ordered dish and with ample reason. First featured in a long-gone New York restaurant called Divan Parisien, this creation combines broccoli and white chicken breasts under a cream sauce blanket. Other favorites are the Fisherman's Prawns and the Sand Dabs, the latter are available only when fresh. Invariably fresh are the vegetables which accompany main courses. For dessert, do not miss the Coeur a la Creme, available nowhere else in town. The ice creams are made on the premises; and you should be of legal age before sampling the rum-riddled Lalla Rookh. The Golden Eagle offers superb creative cooking at moderate prices.

10:30 p.m. Well, if after galavanting all over Japantown, Pacific Heights and Union Street, you are not bushed . . . I am. See you tomorrow.

Your 6th Perfect Day Schedule

9:00 a.m. Easy on breakfast. It is going to be a long fun and food-filled day as we tour the beautiful and historic wine country north of San Francisco.

9:30 a.m. Drive across the majestic Golden Gate Bridge to Sonoma and the Valley of the Moon.

10:30 a.m. Stroll around Sonoma's town square, visiting handcraft shops and viewing buildings dating from California's colorful past.

12:00 noon Your options for lunch today include dining at a superb French country restaurant or picnicking at one of the state's loveliest and most historic wineries.

2:00 p.m. Your tour of the wine country continues as you leave the Valley of the Moon and cross the hills into the famed Napa Valley.

3:45 p.m. Your final winery visit is the most spectacular of all as an aerial tramway carries you to a hilltop complex overlooking the valley below.

6:00 p.m. By taking a highly recommended detour, you can experience the excitement of one of the greatest restaurants in the West, and return via the Bay Bridge with its thrilling view of the San Francisco skyline at night. Or you can drive directly back, stopping to dine in either a uniquely San Francisco institution or in one of our finest Cantonese restaurants.

The Sixth Day of Your
One Perfect Week in San Francisco

9:00 a.m. Weather permitting, this full-day excursion can be the highlight of your San Francisco stay. (Even though it may be foggy in downtown San Francisco, chances are it will be sunny in the wine region.) Featured are the scenic beauties of one of the world's richest wine-producing regions along with delectable accents on food and fine California wines, as well as glimpses of California's past. However, it is a long day, so I advise starting now, perhaps fortified by a very light breakfast at your hotel.

9:30 a.m. Drive out to Van Ness Avenue, a thoroughfare with which by now you should be well acquainted, and head north toward Lombard Street which leads onto the Golden Gate Bridge. Approximately 20 miles along Highway 101 on the Marin County side, turn off onto Highway 37 (marked "Vallejo, Napa"). Seven and a half miles later, turn left onto Highway 121 (marked "Sonoma, Napa"), continuing for another 7 miles. Here, watch for signs leading to Sonoma, turning right and then left 1 mile later onto Highway 12. Proceeding up Highway 12 (now called Broadway), you will soon make out directly ahead the old Sonoma City Hall. However, before you approach the town square, look to the left corner of Broadway and Andreaux where you will spot a yellow building with a sign announcing, Au Relais. Tuck the location of this restaurant in the back of your mind someplace. Now, on arriving at the town square, turn right, locate the nearest free parking space, and begin your walking tour counter-clockwise around the square.

10:30 a.m. Sonoma is a charming little town steeped in early California history. It is the home of the last California mission, the location of the Bear Flag Republic, and the still-intact home of General Vallejo. Luckily, before all visible vestiges of this colorful period of California's past had been eradicated in a post-World War II remodeling fervor, a movement was launched to preserve some of the historic buildings. Therefore, as you stroll around the square, it will not be too difficult to sense what this town was like in the 19th century. However, not all the delights of Sonoma are of yesteryear. As in 1850 when people fled Gold Rush-crazed San Francisco for the calm of Sonoma's lovely valley, young artisans today are drawn to this unhassled, friendly town where they are keepers of small shops in which you will find a wide variety of their handcrafted work.

But before I begin my browsing in any of these stores, I always stop by the Sonoma French Bakery, 470 First Street, next door to the movie theater. Don't be too surprised to find this tiny bakery jam-packed with a line extending onto the sidewalk. Why? Well, as any of those patient patrons will verify, this bakery turns out the finest sourdough French bread in the world! Now, I know that is quite a statement. But it just so happens to be true. And how they do it, no one seems to know. Their other baked goods are quite ordinary. But, the French bread . . . *c'est magnifique!* (By the way, since it is unavailable in San Francisco, any and all city friends would warmly welcome a loaf.)

Continue up First Street. On the far corner, you will find the old mission where, during the fall harvest, the grapes for the new vintage are blessed in a religious ceremony that has been conducted on this spot for years. Now, turn left along Spain Street, the northern perimeter of the square. Here, you will find the barracks which once housed General Vallejo's troops; plus a restored hotel from a later date. Along this street you will also come upon the Sonoma Cheese Factory, 2 West Spain (open daily).

But before you go inside, let me ask what you would like to do for lunch . . . picnic at a historic winery or dine in a beautiful French country restaurant (remember Au Relais, the yellow building?). While it may be too early to actually lunch, you should decide now since Au Relais accepts no reservations at lunch and it can become crowded during the mid-summer months. If a picnic tempts you, let me say that the Sonoma Cheese Factory has just about everything you will need, including some of that fabulous French bread from the Sonoma Bakery. As is only natural in a cheese factory, great emphasis is placed upon cheese and you will find over 100 varieties. Be sure to sample some of their originals—Sonoma Cheddar and Sonoma Jack. You also can buy beer here but who would think of drinking that alien brew in California's beautiful wine country? Wine is the thing and of course, the Cheese Factory has that, too. However, if you are in a picnic mood, I think you'd have more fun if you waited and purchased your wine at the Buena Vista Winery—your luncheon spot—after tasting a few of their offerings.

If you still are not sure about what you want to do for lunch, don't flip a coin. Park yourself on the sidewalk bench and read ahead.

Au Relais, 691 Broadway, Sonoma, (707-996-1031), is a dream of a country restaurant—lovely art-noveau decor, fleet-footed service, superbly prepared dishes from an in-spired and highly original menu. And even though the weather in Sonoma can be pretty hot in the summer (how do you think those plump grapes ripen?), I would not let the heat dampen my appetite or discourage me from taking full advantage of their menu. To start, there is a haunting cold Cucumber and Spinach Soup, an ideal summer refresher. On nippy days, you will find a hot soup, such as their Split Pea, as equally welcome and delicious.

Throughout constant samplings, I have found Au Relais' main courses well nigh infallible. While I usually ignore local prawn dishes because they must of necessity be frozen, I can heartily recommend Au Relais' Prawns Saute Proven-cale cloaked in a light tomato sauce with a mild garlic accent and audaciously flavored with Pernod. Although in France, the great classic Cassoulet—an incomparable stewed medley of beans, sausage, meats and fowls—is generally restricted to winter menus, Au Relais happily dishes up their champion version year round. If you prefer something in the lighter vein, the House Special Crepes are for you: wafer-thin French pancakes hold a mixture of spinach, veal and mushrooms, blanketed by a bechamel sauce and crowned with sweetly stewed tomatoes. But before opting for any of these, inquire if there is any fresh fish on hand. Owner-chef Harry Marsden is a wizard with seafood. And wonder of wonders, most main courses are amply garnished with fresh vegetables cooked ideally *al dente.*

Even when it comes to desserts, Au Relais maintains its stubborn independence from the humdrum by creating novelties such as Beignets, those elegant crullers associated in the U.S. with New Orleans breakfasts; and Diplomat Pudding, a delicate marriage of custard, cake, glazed fruit and creme anglaise. Oh, yes, that almost dessert-rich French bread from the nearby Sonoma Bakery is also on hand, accompanied by its perfect partner, sweet butter. Possibly because the great wine growers are Au Relais habitues—that jolly, heavy-set luncheon regular over there in overalls (custom-made, mind you!) is August Sebastiani whose father founded Sebastiani Vineyards in 1865—the wine list reads like a "What's What" of California wines, with some of their imported brethren to boot! Moderate prices, considering the incredible expertise.

Now, with the "where to lunch" question resolved, you can go inside the Sonoma Cheese Factory and shop around a bit and/or head down Broadway to Au Relais if reading about all that luscious food has made you hungry. First, though, while you are in the area, you may wish to visit General Vallejo's home, part of the State Department of Parks (small admission). In this Gothic Revival house, you will view rooms just as they were in the late 1800's, replete with Victorian furnishings brought around the Horn. On the hillside above the house is a lovely shaded artesian-fed reservoir, which gave the property its name, *Lachryma Montis* or "tears of the mountain."

If you are going picnicking and have your provisions in

hand, drive to the southeast corner of the square where you will find a sign pointing out "Napa Street, to the Buena Vista Winery." Keep driving along Napa Street until you cross some railroad tracks (about 1 mile), turning left immediately thereafter.

In a few minutes you will find yourself in an idyllic setting which is not only an active winery with tree-shaded tables outside for your luncheon comfort, but a historic spot as well. It was here that General Vallejo first planted grapes in 1832. But it was not until the arrival of a Hungarian nobleman, Count Agoston Haraszthy, that the Buena Vista was established as one of the first wineries in California. After searching the West for over a decade in order to locate a suitable climate in which the grape-cuttings of his native Hungary would flourish, the Count discovered the Sonoma area or, as the Indians called it, the Valley of the Moon. Here he settled, striking up a close friendship-rivalry with General Vallejo (who was a proud amateur vintner) and by 1857, bottled his first pressings.

Because of his pioneering work in what is now one of California's most famous industries, Haraszthy has been officially recognized as "The Father of California Viticulture." The vine-covered stone building on your right dates from this early period of California's wine history. Stepping into its cool interior, you can take a short self-guided wine tour, terminating at a tasting room back in the mountainside cellars, dug by Chinese laborers over a century ago. In the tasting room, you may sample some of the Buena Vista's current output.

No matter if you decided to lunch "al fresco" here or inside Au Relais' charming restaurant, the Buena Vista Winery is a "must-see." And be sure to buy a bottle of the Green Hungarian. It is most appropriate for toasting old Count Haraszthy anytime, anyplace.

2:00 p.m. Time to tear yourself away from either Au Relais' Gallic creations or your picnic spread and wend your way back to Sonoma's town square, where you should continue out Napa Street to the west this time. Following the Highway 12 markers toward Santa Rosa, you will soon pass through small towns such as Boyes Springs, Fetters Springs and Agua Caliente, names harkening back to when this area supported many spas, fed by hot mineral springs from the nearby mountains. But keep a careful eye open for a sign indicating "Trinity Road—Oakville." Turn right here and almost instantly, you will find yourself climbing a ridge of mountains with over-the-shoulder views of the Valley of the Moon behind you. Remain on the Oakville Grade and you will abruptly top the crest. Before you, in sweeping panorama, lies the fertile Napa Valley. Visitors who have never toured wine-producing areas are often shocked to discover that in late fall, grape leaves turn into the flaming red, deep orange, and purple of New England's fall foliage. Should this be the time of your visit, this view is all the more awesome.

Proceed down the grade to Highway 29, turn left and you are in the very heart of the great Napa Valley. If you are at all cognizant of California wines, the next several miles north will be mind-boggling. Concentrated along this road are some of the most famous names in California wine-making—Beaulieu, Inglenook, Robert Mondavi, Beringer, Charles Krug—all with tasting rooms! In order to weed out the Sunday imbiber from the more serious wine taster-purchaser, many wineries have been forced to insist visitors take a tour prior to entering the tasting room. Therefore, the number of wineries you visit and how much wine you sample is up to you. But watch the clock. Our last scheduled winery is Sterling Vineyards, 1 mile south of Calistoga off Highway 29. Another one of our "must-see's," it closes at 4:30 p.m. which means you should arrive there about 4:00 p.m.

3:45 p.m. Well, time to head further north to the far end of the Napa Valley and Sterling Vineyards. After passing the Napa Valley State Park on your left, start watching for a cluster of white buildings on a hilltop to your right. Once in sight, you may think that somehow the stark white struc-

tures of an Aegean Island have been magically transported
to a California landscape. (Camera buffs take note: You
will be leaving the winery via a different route. Therefore,
this unique view will not come again.) Just when you think
you have missed the turnoff, you will see a sign indicating
"Dunaweal Lane, to Sterling Vineyards" and others direct-
ing you to the visitors' parking area. Here, at the hill's base,
is an aerial tramway which will silently carry you up to the
winery for a $2.00 per person charge. It is worth every cent.
For at the summit, you can conduct yourself through one of
the newest and most beautiful wineries in the state. Actually,
the interior is comparable to a contemporary museum with
ancient and modern art depicting all phases of wine-making.
Each step of the process is clearly explained and the actual
machinery is visible.

Yet, not even this impressive tour can compete with the
vista of the surrounding lush valley. I have intentionally
scheduled your arrival here late in the day when most of
the visitors have departed. At this more quiet time, the
winery takes on a monastic air. And when the many bells
—originally from St. Dunstans Church in London—peel out
from their towers, it is a moment to remember.

Naturally, wine tastings are available in a handsome lounge
or on a sunny patio. Out-of-staters can be somewhat frustrated if they become attached to Sterling wines as they are
difficult to locate in most liquor stores. Sterling prefers to
reserve much of their output for purchasers at the winery
and for diners in finer restaurants. For example, I have found
some Sterling wines on the Four Seasons' extremely impressive list in New York.

6:00 p.m. Well, time to leave the tranquility of this marvelous white aerie, and press on. So glide back to the valley
floor via the tramway and exit from the winery, this time
to the right. Soon, another right will head you back down
the Napa Valley, not on Highway 29 but rather on the lesser
traveled Silverado Trail. And as you drive along, you can
be thinking about where to dine—this time for dinner. My

strongest recommendation is that you take a slight detour to one of the greatest restaurants in the West. After all, if you were traversing the French wine region following that bible of gastronomy, the *Guide Michelin,* you would certainly search out three-star restaurants which the *Guide* equates with being "worthy of a special journey." Well, in my book, the Nut Tree is certainly one.

The Nut Tree, Interstate 80 near Vacaville, (707-448-6411; reservations accepted for any day except Sundays and holidays), is far more than one of the greatest restaurants in California. It is an experience for the eye! Throughout the building—which also includes a fantastic merchandise area—are masterpieces of color and design on its walls, on its tables, everywhere you turn your head. In the shopping section, I am always taken by an enormous wall display of kitchen utensils arrayed like a sunburst while an army of ever-ready gingerbread men in rainbow-hued icings never fails to make me smile. Nowhere have I seen such a collection of tasteful gift items and household accessories presented with such genius.

And this same genius extends into the vast dining room. There, I always request a table on the far side of the walk-through aviary, filled with exotically plumed birds. Children in your party may delight over a mobile of an ancient aircraft suspended from the high ceiling, while you may be enchanted with the never-ending borders of bright fresh flowers and wall hangings, such as a collage of dolls. The whole color scheme of the room changes with the seasons and it always possesses a fresh, breezy feeling.

At this point, you may be thinking: "Sure, I've been in restaurants with brilliant decor, but the food left much to be desired." Well, the Nut Tree is *the* exception—and that's why it is so great! I can't tell you how often I have breakfasted, lunched and dined at the Nut Tree over the years, but I can tell you that never—yes, that is *never*—have I found a canned or frozen fruit or vegetable. As with the finest restaurants in France, what is available changes with the season. And during those few months when fresh produce is at its low point even in bountiful California, the Nut Tree flies some in from Hawaii and further.

Take plenty of time to peruse the multi-paged menu where each dish is fully explained, not in that glossy "come-on" menuese so prevalent today, but in basic, plain English. As you leaf through its pages, you will realize that the Nut Tree is uniquely Western in its culinary orientation. Our state's Mexican heritage is acknowledged by an authentic cornhusk Tamale, created from a recipe which is often imitated but remains unmatched. Served with it are California's own Monterey jack cheese and a halved avocado, stuffed with marinated lima beans. Now what could be more California? Totally superb! Our Chinese influence is presented in a delicious Tomato-Beef dish which might not be as authentic as you would find in the better Chinatown restaurants, but it is handled extremely well and is refreshingly devoid of those inexpensive "stretchers" like hunks of celery.

As much as I admire the Nut Tree's cooking skills, when summer comes, I don't even open the menu . . . for visions of their Fresh Fruit Plate have danced in my head all winter long. If you are a fruit fancier and this is indeed the season —you have just found utopia! Servings of every imaginable fruit, berry and melon are artfully arranged on your plate in the center of which is your choice of cottage cheese or ice cream. I rather doubt you will ever see its like elsewhere. (Luckily, smaller fruit plates serve as first courses on some regular dinners.) The same accolade can be lavished on their Italian Vegetable Salad which includes a portion of fresh string beans in a marinade that is ambrosial. If you crave something more in the sandwich line, try the Nut Tree's hot Turkey and Ham on Crumpet Bread, bathed in a cheese sauce. For desserts, I grow weak at the thought of their Banana Praline Sundae. An exceptional selection of teas, imported beers and fine California wines is on hand. But then I would expect or accept nothing less from the exceptional Nut Tree.

Now that I hope your appetite is sufficiently whetted, let me tell you how to get to the Nut Tree. Simply proceed down the Silverado Trail about 12 miles from Sterling Winery. Turn left at Highway 128 and drive over the hills, then through 39 miles of rich fruit orchards to Winters. At Winters, turn onto 505 (a divided freeway) following the signs to Vacaville. Eleven miles later, take the exit marked "Sacramento, Highway 80 East," but immediately on making that exit, turn off onto a frontage road to the right. There you will spot the Nut Tree Airport. (Yes, it has its own airport, post office and even zip code!) Turn left at the sign indicating "Food and Hotel."

After dining at the Nut Tree, simply pull onto Interstate 80 to San Francisco. It is multi-lane freeway all the way back through the East Bay and across the Bay Bridge into San Francisco. If it is a clear night, the view of the San Francisco skyline from the upper deck of the bridge is one you will remember as the perfect ending to a perfect day.

If, on the other hand, all the wining and driving has taken its toll on your energies and you simply cannot face the detour to the Nut Tree, you can drive directly back to San Francisco from Sterling Winery by continuing down the Silverado Trail (*not* turning left at Highway 128) for another 13 miles. Here the Silverado dead ends at Trancas Street. Turn right for 2 miles, then left onto Highway 29 (marked "Vallejo"). Now follow Highway 121 signs which will lead you into Highway 37. Highway 37 will lead you directly to Highway 101 south to San Francisco, which is the route we started north on this morning.

While traveling back to San Francisco, you might wish to consider having dinner at one of two restaurants. They have been purposely included in today's schedule for not one but three very important reasons: both offer superb food; both are easily accessible from the route you must take to reach downtown San Francisco (no need to change your clothes, casual attire perfectly acceptable); and both offer a simplicity which would ideally cap this long day.

Marin Joe's, 1585 Casa Buena Drive off Highway 101, Corte Madera, (924-2081), is one of a breed of restaurants indigenous to San Francisco. To any resident, a "Joe's" restaurant immediately means an open charcoal grill, a heavily Italian-accented menu with equal emphasis on steaks and chops, and counter as well as booth service. San Francisco still boasts several Joe's, yet today, the mantle of "top Joe's" rests securely on the shoulders of this Marin County roadside operation. Here, frozen vegetables are shunned (except for an occasional appearance in the mixed-vegetable garnish) and shortcuts, such as powdered stock concentrates in the minestrone, are abhorred. What you find is good, wholesome, down-to-earth cooking, expertly done by a team of chefs who work with dazzling elan. Their performance is best witnessed from a ringside counter seat.

Start with a cup or bowl of Marin Joe's fine minestrone, followed by either a Rib Steak (that old-fashioned, deliciously juicy cut so seldom found on today's menus) or their extra-thick Lamb Chops (medium rare, of course). Naturally, be certain you specify your steak or chops be charcoal broiled. The pastas are also quite fine but you must request that they be cooked to order, *al dente,* for which you pay a slight premium.

Side orders of vegetables play important roles in any Joe's meal, especially at Marin Joe's where they are fresh. Therefore, I always ask that the mixed vegetables which come with the meat courses be replaced (at a slight charge) by either Swiss chard, Italian beans, zucchini or spinach. All these vegetables have been parboiled in advance. However, each order is sauteed to order in olive oil with a touch of garlic, arriving at your table piping hot and delicious.

One dish that every Joe's and only a Joe's features is the Joe's Special. Legend has it that late one night many years ago, a group of regulars arrived at a Joe's to find the kitchen's food supply almost depleted. All the chef could stir up were some eggs, ground beef, onions and leftover parboiled spinach. Well, stir them up he did, scrambling them into a concoction that is neither scrambled eggs nor omelette but strictly San Franciscan! Marin Joe's adds fresh sliced mushrooms for an elegant touch on request.

Desserts are almost non-existent except for a sensational

Zabaione, that frothy Italian delight of whipped eggs and Marsala wine. I prefer Marin Joe's version to any in San Francisco's far more de luxe and expensive restaurants. But then, quality takes center stage here, not elaborate service or fancified decor. And there are countless San Franciscans willing to drive across the Golden Gate and encounter a possible wait for a table, just to indulge in the finest example of this uniquely San Francisco style of dining. Moderate prices.

To reach Marin Joe's as you drive south towards San Francisco on Highway 101, after San Rafael start watching for a turnoff to the right marked "Corte Madera-Larkspur." Take this exit and proceed to the first stoplight, keeping to the far left. Turn left onto Casa Buena which runs parallel to the freeway. Marin Joe's is on the right. After dinner, all you need do to reach San Francisco is continue south on Casa Buena and in a few minutes, you will be able to re-enter the freeway, heading to the Golden Gate Bridge and your hotel.

The other dinner suggestion is: Mike's Chinese Cuisine, 5145 Geary Boulevard at 16th Avenue, (752-0120). Mike's is a great Chinese restaurant. It is also a rather unusual one. Unlike the majority of its Cantonese counterparts who offer a minimum of 150 different selections, Mike's menu is very brief. And while all too many Chinatown places continue to add more and more inexpensive ingredients, such as huge chunks of celery, onion and bamboo, to stretch dishes and keep costs down, Mike's does not hesitate in raising prices while keeping the quality pristine. Furthermore, whereas the rotation of chefs in large establishments, especially those open for lunch and dinner, often makes Chinese dining a variation of Russian roulette, at Mike's, Mike is personally in the kitchen just about every night and therefore, the consistency is practically unfailing.

Mike's style of clear, unencumbered cooking is apparent in my perennial first course, an ethereal Mustard Green Soup —sparkling clear broth, brilliantly green under-done mustard greens, tender filets of pork and a shred of ginger. The delicate sweetness of the superb stock and tender pork contrasted with the quasi-bitterness of the mustard greens represents, to me, the quintessence of Cantonese cuisine. My second course is usually the Chicken Salad, that compelling mixture of shredded chicken, lettuce, coriander and onions. Then, if you fancy sweet and sour pork, meet the San Francisco champion: Sweet and Sour Pork de Luxe. Cubes of tender pork, batter dipped and fried to insure the proper outer crispness, are bathed in a luxuriant sauce rich with translucent pieces of preserved melon, pineapple cubes, and gingery delicacies. The Paper Wrapped Chicken is another favorite, while the Crystal Shrimp (quickly stir-fried so they all but explode in your mouth) are brilliant. If, like me, you simply cannot get enough of the refreshing clean flavors of Chinese vegetables, then try the Tenderloin with Chinese Greens, or the Beef with Sugar Pea Pods.

End your dinner, as most Chinese would, with a stellar Steamed Rock Cod, its silk-smooth sweet flakes gently flavored by ginger, onion, coriander and soy sauce. That should ring down the curtain on a perfect Cantonese dinner! And should you return here next year, you would find the exact same undulled freshness, expert flavor balance, and stylistic simplicity. No, it hasn't been a dream: it was just dinner at Mike's. Moderate prices.

How to reach Mike's? Cross the Golden Gate Bridge into San Francisco. A few hundred yards past the toll plaza, curve to the right following the signs to 19th Avenue and Golden Gate Park which, via a tunnel, will whisk you through the Presidio. At the fourth stoplight (Geary Street), turn right for two blocks and you will find Mike's on the left-hand side of the street. After dining, all you need do is head down Geary in the opposite direction from which you arrived. Geary will take you directly downtown.

10:30 p.m. Well, whether you dined at the Nut Tree, Marin Joe's or Mike's Chinese Cuisine, you now should be back at your hotel . . . probably just as bushed as I am. However, if you're not (bushed, that is), all I can say is any carousing you want to do after a day like this will have to be done on your own! Good night. See you tomorrow.

Your 7th Perfect Day Schedule

9:00 a.m. Indulge yourself with a sumptuous breakfast feast at a bit of old Vienna as you launch your last day in San Francisco.

10:00 a.m. Either tie up all those last-day loose ends or relax aboard a cruise ship and tour the Bay, seeing San Francisco from an exciting, different perspective.

12:00 noon A lavish buffet high atop a Nob Hill tower or a delicious Japanese lunch in a downtown "find"—those are your two distinctly different choices.

2:00 p.m. It's a free afternoon. Enjoy it by revisiting and resavoring your favorite corner of San Francisco.

6:30 p.m. With the city at your feet, sip a farewell cocktail in one of our high-in-the-sky rooms.

8:00 p.m. A final elegant dinner at either the city's most chic French dining room or in an intimate clubby hideway, or experience a great San Francisco culinary tradition—the "complete Italian dinner" in North Beach.

10:30 p.m. If you are heading home tomorrow morning, or are setting out on one of the exciting side trips detailed in Part Two of this book, you had better call it an evening. So until I see you in San Francisco again, *au revoir, auf Wiedersehen, arrivederci*—so long.

The Seventh Day of Your
One Perfect Week in San Francisco

9:00 a.m. Good morning! Well, this could be your last full day in San Francisco. Therefore, I purposely have framed a very loose format for you today. I know that whenever I enjoy a week or more in any one city, I invariably find that on my last day, there are many loose ends to take care of, such as returning the rental car, picking up purchases held at stores, firing off a few last postcards, etc. Also, there are favored places to revisit, to resavor before leaving. And for you, today is that last day to fit it all in.

You will need breakfast to carry you through the morning of what can be a busy day, so why not make it a very good one at the Vienna Coffee House, Hotel Mark Hopkins, Mason and California Streets, (392-3434). Here you can hedonistically indulge yourself in a luxurious, multi-coursed feast, or show great restraint with only juice, coffee and a piece of pastry. No matter what you choose, you cannot go wrong. To start, you can request, at a premium price, squeezed-to-order orange juice (not listed on the menu). The grilled, thick ham steak is beautifully tender and delicately sugar-cured sweet, while the pancakes possess a real buttermilk sourness, rendering them irresistible. Or, for something rarely encountered in this country, try the Danish Ableskivers, apple slices encased in pancake batter, baked to a golden brown, and dusted with powdered sugar. Heighten your enjoyment of them with boysenberry or maple syrup, just as you would with pancakes.

Although the pancakes and ableskivers are tempting, bypass them if you think they may preclude your ordering one of the Vienna Coffee House's truly outstanding pastries. A different one is available each day; for example, on Thursday, there is the sumptuous Kaese Schmitten, a lovely raisin-studded puff-paste crust holding a light, vaguely sweet, cheese filling. Fabled Demel's in old Vienna would be proud to serve its equal! And wonder of wonders, the coffee is remarkably good, thereby destroying San Francisco's almost perfect record of miserable breakfast brews. If you fancy hot chocolate, this is the place for it—made with milk, *not* water, and lavishly heaped with whipped cream in true Viennese fashion. A totally delicious breakfast which can be costly in calories as well as dollars.

10:00 a.m. The impatient clanging of a cable car passing by on California Street might be just the incentive required to arouse you from your euphoria. Outside, San Francisco waits to say good-bye.

For those of you who have tied up all those loose ends and wish to experience another facet of San Francisco this morning, I am not about to abandon you. Why not enjoy your last perfect morning in San Francisco on San Francisco Bay? All you need do is walk one block down California Street to Powell and catch a cable car of the Powell Street line (yellow sign on the roof and front), headed toward Fisherman's Wharf. Ride it to the end of the line at Bay Street and proceed directly ahead to the Wharf where, at Pier 43½, you will come upon a ship of the Red & White Fleet ready to take you on a 1¼-hour Bay cruise. (These cruise ships depart at 10:00 a.m. daily, at 30 to 45-minute intervals thereafter, depending on the time of year. Telephone 398-1141 for specific times.)

On board and under way, you will turn westward toward the Golden Gate. From either the warmth of the enclosed lower deck or from the breeze-swept top deck, you can watch the San Francisco skyline pass in review. First, Fisherman's Wharf with Russian Hill in the background; then Fort Mason and the Marina with its row of luxury homes overlooking the yacht harbor. A taped narration, gratefully bereft of those lame puns and stale jokes which afflict most tour talks, will call your attention to points of interest ashore.

You will be acquainted with many of the landmarks, such
as the Palace of Fine Arts and Fort Point, having already
visited them earlier in your stay. But the Bay cruise places
them in a different, overall perspective, set against the backdrop of the city's hills and, hopefully, a brilliant blue sky.
Soon, your cruise ship will timidly poke its prow under the
Golden Gate Bridge, gracefully arching high overhead, and
hastily turn back from the choppy waters of the entrance
to the smoother Bay itself. Within a few minutes, you will
be gliding by Alcatraz, now deserted except for bands of
curious visitors traipsing through the vacant cellblocks. On
the port side, you will see Treasure Island, site of the 1939
World's Fair and now a U.S. Navy base. If some of the
buildings appear a bit grandiose for a naval installation, it
is just that they are remnants of the Fair's exotic architecture. A quick swing under the massive Bay Bridge and you
begin your return back along the Embarcadero and the Ferry
Building. Here, the exciting skyline of downtown San Francisco towers high above the Bay. It is a marvelously impressive sight.

12:00 noon By now you will have docked at Fisherman's
Wharf. And unless you wish to revisit The Cannery or Ghirardelli Square, I suggest you head back downtown. To do
so, just climb aboard a cable car at the Bay and Taylor
Streets turntable.

For lunch, I have two distinctly different suggestions. Your
choice between them will be based, no doubt, on the quantity you consumed at breakfast. Probably not even the Bay's
appetite-whetting breezes could entice you to face an enormous buffet lunch if you threw caution to the wind at the
Vienna Coffee House. But . . . let me see if I can tempt you,
anyway.

The Crown Room, Fairmont Hotel, Mason and California Streets, (772-5131), is perched on the uppermost level
of the Fairmont Tower on Nob Hill and offers luncheon goers
the most impressive buffet in town. Actually, buffets can be
the bane of any food critic's life. It has become painfully

apparent that the vast majority of chefs who prepare buffets are seriously infected by the "dazzle them with quantity" virus and are totally impervious to the "it's quality, not quantity" antidote. The most noticeable talent these so-called chefs display is their ability to operate a can opener, as evidenced by endless bowls of canned fruit, assorted olives and artless tuna salads. I, therefore, usually avoid buffets like the plague! Luckily for you, however, the Crown Room buffet is a remarkable exception. First of all, this buffet is extremely high on fresh, top-quality ingredients. Gleaming bowls of fresh papaya, pineapple, berries in season, etc. greet the diner. Secondly, there is no skimping on the more costly foods; copious platters of smoked salmon, delicate Bay shrimp, and pink roast beef are almost always part of the lavish display.

And when canned ingredients such as artichoke bottoms, tinned fish and other buffet standards are used, each is touched with creativity by intriguing vinaigrettes or sauces, or mixed in palate-pleasing combinations which offer a striking parade of delightful flavors and textures. The Fairmont's chef also demonstrates his aptitude in his selection of the types of hot dishes that can best survive the debilitating environment of steam tables. For example, a succulent roast pork loin stuffed with prunes and served with red cabbage, was an ideal buffet hot dish on my last visit. To climax your lunch, the baked desserts, served from a laden cart, are exceptional. All this, in addition to an outside elevator ride, plus an incredible 360-degree view of San Francisco, makes lunch at the Crown Room a totally delightful experience.

If, however, you do not wish to spare the time for a lengthy, relaxed and somewhat costly lunch, then I suggest Midori, 352 Grant Avenue at Bush, (982-3546). Conveniently located within a block of the downtown shopping hub, Midori caters mainly to Japan Airline crews who stop over at an adjacent hotel, and knowledgeable business people from the nearby financial district who appreciate both the excellent, authentic Japanese cuisine and the very reasonable prices.

One of the outstanding characteristics of Midori is that the menu changes daily. In this way, the kitchen is not fettered to the same dishes day in and day out; the availability of fresh ingredients and the whim of the chef dictate the choices. The day's repertory is scribbled on an index card in often rather odd-sounding literal translations from the Japanese. This functional but informal menu typifies the casualness of Midori's service. But there is nothing in the least casual about the cooking! One frequently recurring specialty is Ginger-yaki, excellent quality beef strips, glazed with a titillating soy-ginger sauce similar to what you find on most teriyaki dishes, but far more expert. In season, the Salmon-yaki is glorious. It is broiled without the use of fat or butter; instead, salt is used in a uniquely Japanese cooking technique called "shioyaki." Gyoza, those meat-filled dumplings you may have encountered at Sanppo, are featured fairly regularly. Here, they are more pungent with garlic, yet absolutely delicious. Midori usually offers at least one traditional "donburi" each day. Donburi is a popular Japanese one-dish meal combining meat, eggs, and vegetables fried into an omelette and served over rice. My favorite is the one which the menu lists as Pork Cutlet, Vegetables and Eggs on Rice. Except during summer and fall when they somehow manage to come up with the most exquisite California melons, Midori offers no desserts. Inexpensive and excellent!

2:00 p.m. I have nothing specific planned for you this afternoon; as the tour brochures would say, it is a "free afternoon." Perhaps you want to fill it by revisiting your favorite San Francisco places, by strolling through Chinatown once again, by dropping in at that museum which you just didn't give enough time to, by sitting contentedly in Golden Gate Park and soaking in its beauty and freedom. Or, you might wish to do a bit more shopping with an eye towards finding something to take home with you as a suitable memento of your San Francisco stay . . . something that will recapture for you the look and feel of the city. Why not drop into a bookstore and ask for a copy of *Above San Francisco, Volume II,* published by Cameron & Company? This breathtaking volume of color photographs presents San Francisco in all her glory as seen by a swooping gull or jet pilot. Dazzlingly photographed from above, in a clarity which rivals that rare light of the Aegean Islands, this is San Francisco as we who live here like to think of her . . . and as we hope you will remember her. Back home, it will help you answer the inevitable question asked by family and friends, "What is San Francisco?" And I, too, would like to add my thoughts on that question.

What is San Francisco?

Columnists and authors have pondered this for years and the library is packed with their varied conclusions. There are even entire books devoted to this one subject. To follow in the wake of such illustrious company is daring, but I do not feel this book would be complete without an attempt. So here I go, throwing caution to the wind.

To understand the lure and charm of San Francisco, we must first destroy a myth. That myth is the notion that San Francisco is a "second New York." Nothing could be further from the truth. San Francisco and New York are completely different, regardless of what you have heard. For sheer facilities, art museums, theaters, restaurants, and every other diversion, there is no city in America to compete with New York. However, for sheer charm, atmosphere, and a modest but sufficient number of facilities, San Francisco has no peer.

It is impossible to answer the question, "What is San Francisco?" without falling into a kind of flowery, self-conscious prose which defeats its own purpose. I have never read a good description of San Francisco. And not wishing to follow failure with failure, I will attempt to answer the question, "What is San Francisco?" by simply summing up the city's outstanding points.

A City in the Country. San Francisco is in the unique and fortunate position of offering its residents and visitors many of the facilities of a great metropolis without forcing them to sacrifice their natural love of greenery and fresh air. It is a city of views, of shiny leaves, of sunsets, of water, of God's green earth. In New York City, for instance, it is quite possible to live in Brooklyn or Queens and to travel back and forth to work in Manhattan by subway and never, except by chance, see any expanse of water or groves of trees. Not so in San Francisco.

The very heart of the shopping district on Market Street provides one with a clear view of Twin Peaks. The top of elegant Nob Hill provides a view of rural Marin County. And the cable car ride provides views of Oakland and Berkeley.

Relatively Uncrowded. As cities go, San Francisco is relatively uncrowded. Some of our city bus users might argue this point, but that is because they haven't seen other cities. For example, commuter buses cannot leave the terminals with standees. Contrast this with some of the sardine-packed transportation of New York and you will agree that San Francisco is not crowded.

A Sense of Humor. With fewer annoyances than are encountered in other large metropolitan areas, San Franciscans don't take themselves too seriously! Although civic pride is never in short supply, they like nothing better than to kid their city, its officials, and most of all—themselves. San Franciscans can take a good joke on themselves, though they can view such things as civic malpractice with great seriousness.

Views for Rent. As a "city in the country," San Francisco is a "city of views" also. Apartments are rented more on the basis of their views than on their spaciousness. Thus, a one-room studio with a sweeping panorama of the Bay may rent for a much higher figure than a six-room flat whose view is the wall of another building.

A White City. The cluster of tall, downtown buildings makes a view worth seeing, for San Francisco is a white city. Visitors who have been to Chicago or New York almost always make this their first observation. One can see the whiteness of the city by merely driving across the Golden Gate Bridge. The homes and buildings of San Francisco, particularly on a sunny day, have a just-scrubbed look about them which continually delights the visitor.

Character and "Characters." All in all, San Francisco is truly a city of character. The things I have described above give the city its special quality. But, in addition, the city is the proud possessor of many creative and unusual individuals, some of whom might be called "characters" elsewhere. San Francisco does not merely tolerate its characters; it encourages them. Perhaps as a result of this, creative individualism can flourish here longer than elsewhere.

Daily Courtesy. San Franciscans take pride in their day-to-day courtesy. There are exceptions, of course. But by and large, waitresses, clerks, even bus drivers, and especially the wonderful breed of cable-car gripmen dispense courteous treatment freely to the public. Simply purchasing a loaf of bread in a busy bakery will often find kind words or small talk exchanged between customer and clerk. And visitors from large Eastern cities are always amazed at the courteous treatment by taxi drivers, famous elsewhere for their rudeness.

Will It Last? Will the uniqueness and individuality of San Francisco last? Every day finds real estate interests tearing down the old and putting up the new. Will San Francisco change?

Of course, the city will change—it is constantly changing. What doesn't? But fortunately, the changes will be slower here, and the changes will encounter more opposition than elsewhere. So, if you can't make your visit to San Francisco this year, you may be assured that whenever you do come, you will find most of the things described above, as well as those indefinable qualities not even named, pretty much the same. And once you have made your acquaintance with our beautiful fair city, you will have your own true answer to the question: "What is San Francisco?"

6:30 p.m. Where will it be for cocktails this evening? Perhaps a return to the Top of the Mark to watch it grow dark, or another go around of the Equinox Room, or maybe you would like to sample a different room-with-a-view, the one high atop the St. Francis Hotel Tower called Victor's. A high-powered outside elevator propels you above Union Square in a matter of seconds. Once seated in one of the semi-secluded alcoves, you can gaze out over the entire downtown area, the Bay and the East Bay hills beyond. Whichever view room you choose, the city lying at your feet will now, I hope, seem a very familiar place, filled with a great many memories to cherish.

8:00 p.m. If it was difficult for me to select from among all our great restaurants the ones to offer you on your first perfect day, the choice is equally challenging for tonight. Not only do I want to provide the finest in cuisine, but also the appropriate atmosphere for that true San Francisco finale. Of the three I have decided upon, two are quite expensive and elegant, while the third is more casual, moderately priced yet no less excellent in its old-fashioned way.

Although I steadfastly refuse to name any one San Francisco restaurant as *the* best, I have no reluctance to dub L'Etoile, 1075 California Street, (771-1529; reservations imperative), the most chic. From the moment you step into its lengthy foyer and descend the sweeping staircase, you know you have entered a special place. The interior is inspired, the creation of Michael Taylor, one of the city's most renowned decorators. The scale of the room, the profusion of flowers held in gigantic urns, and the lighting's roseate glow create a gentle splendor evocative of Europe's most exalted dining salons. Little wonder that this impeccable environment is so often chosen as the setting for social soirees that are the province of *Town & Country* and *Women's Wear Daily*. Yet, when a restaurant achieves this kind of eminence among the elite, it often turns its attention away from the kitchen. Not so with L'Etoile. As this restaurant increased in prominence, the kitchen gained in stature. Today, its cuisine can be ranked among the finest in town.

Naturally, as with any restaurant, some of L'Etoile's dishes are more brilliant than others. And to me, one of the crowning achievements is the Coquilles St. Jacques a la Nage. Because there are no Western Scallops, these are jetted in from the East Coast and therefore, are not always available. But ask. If you are fortunate, you will be presented a serving of infinitely delicate, snow-white beauties, cooked for just a few moments in a carrot-and-onion enriched court-bouillon, and then napped in a fragile beurre blanc (white butter sauce). If the scallops missed the last plane out of Boston, do not bemoan your fate—instead, order the Homard Roi George (for two as a first course), a triumphant alliance of lobster meat, mushrooms and shrimp in a haunting port-wine sauce.

As for the main course, I suggest you ask your captain what he considers especially fine that evening which would appropriately follow your choice of first course. Too many diners commit a "cardinal ordering sin" by electing an elaborate main course to follow a very complex first course. For example, if I had the refreshingly simple scallops, then I would opt for something like one of L'Etoile's richly sauced veal dishes. However, if my first course was the opulent lobster, then I would be inclined toward a simpler meat, perhaps their blushing-pink rack of lamb discreetly accompanied by some simple fresh vegetables. In French cuisine, balance is a prime requisite to full enjoyment.

To clear the palate, I would relish an uncomplicated fresh green salad. Then . . . roll out the pastry cart! The acquisition of an outstanding pastry chef has been greeted as the latest star in the L'Etoile constellation. On my last visit, I lost myself in an extravagant chocolate cake! As a separate course, a full-bodied, filtered coffee would follow. Then, to further mellow my mood, I would order a snifter of cognac in the bar where some of the finest piano playing can be heard this side of the Opera House stage. Stellar performances by the decorator, dining room staff, kitchen and pianist in a total dining experience which lives up to its name—*the star.*

Le Club, 1250 Jones Street, (771-5400; reservations imperative), is another de luxe restaurant which gives full measure to its name. Nestled off the lobby of a posh Nob Hill apartment house, this intimate hideaway is replete with the aura of an exclusive club—it even pampers its guests with touches like matchbooks imprinted with their names when reservations are placed at least a day in advance.

While Le Club's kitchen may not readily soar into the rarified "haute cuisine" stratosphere achieved by some of L'Etoile's classics, it presents an eclectic menu of exceedingly well-handled dishes, with emphasis on the finest of ingredients. For example, their fish is purchased from the city's foremost retail purveyor, so be certain to ask if that evening's fresh fish offering might be suitable to be split for two as a first course, such as the poached salmon. Failing this, the escargots and the sauteed prawns are both masterfully prepared.

For a main course, Le Club seems to ferret out the very youngest, most tender lamb and treats it with the respect it deserves, garnishing it handsomely with a mini-garden of beautifully prepared vegetables. And because of Le Club's high purchasing standards, this is certainly the place to order veal. On the other hand, chicken—especially the Breast of Capon with Cognac and Chestnuts—should not be overlooked. The flawlessly prepared chicken retains a succulence truly remarkable in light of today's cardboard-textured birds.

Desserts are made on the premises and run the gamut from an impressive St. Honore Cake, that pastry chef's homage to the patron saint of bakers, to a satiny-smooth, aristocratic Bread Pudding, far removed from its plebian background. Cafe filtre is the harmonious coda to this dinner. But don't rush off. The grand finale should be a cognac or glass of port in the intimate bar, where the maitre d's English accent will help you fantasize that you are, indeed, in some private British club where everything runs in a time-honored, smooth fashion. Expensive.

Swiss Louis, 493 Broadway, (421-2913), is a holdover from a once-great San Francisco dining tradition—the "complete Italian dinners." Throughout this book, you will note that, with few exceptions, I stress ordering a la carte. And I do so because most "complete dinners" are illusions— that is, a vapid soup and limp salad haphazardly appended to a main course. At one time, true "complete dinners" were a great and respected San Francisco culinary tradition. North Beach restaurants rivaled one another in laying before diners stupendous spreads of outstanding quality. As time passed, some of the exponents of this family style of dining went highbrow. An example of this is the internationally known Ernie's. Today, Ernie's looks upon its Italian "complete dinner" heritage with seeming disdain, and instead serves inane, fancified, Frenchified cooking. Other once-famed "complete dinner" restaurants now cling only to a sparse skeleton of this former glorious tradition. But in Swiss Louis, the "complete dinner" in the bountiful, grand manner is still alive and well.

Your first course will be a mammoth tray of Italian hors d'oeuvres—prosciutto, mortadella, copa, salami, marinated artichokes, anchovies, black and green olives, celery, scal-. lions, pepperoni, and ceci . . . "a meal in itself," to quote my mother. This spread is equally impressive in quality as well as quantity! Plenty of fresh French bread is on hand; and served almost simultaneously is a provocative green salad enhanced by Bay shrimp and tossed with a sprightly dressing which crosses a Louis (no relation) dressing with a vinaigrette. This is followed by a homemade soup, usually filled with fresh vegetables.

In selecting your main course, you will require my assistance in interpreting the menu. You see, Swiss Louis has such a devoted following of "old-timers," the menu makes no attempt to sell; rather, it just lists items in the most mundane terms. For example, "Broiled Chicken" is the designation for the rarely found Pollo Schiacciato, a half chicken compressed in a heavy iron framework and then broiled. This process results in a more uniformly crisped skin and a juicier interior. The "Fried Prawns" are lightly fried and bask in a lively wine-lemon sauce, far removed from those batter-laden presentations. Even some of the steaks are treated to unusual "house" preparations. All main courses are garnished by flavorful fresh vegetables. Keeping alive another old tradition, Swiss Louis then serves a cheese course with an abundant basket of fresh fruit and nuts for dessert. After a feast like this, the cleansing acidity of a fresh orange or the natural sweetness of an apple fills the bill. Moderate, surprisingly so.

10:30 p.m.   The time has come to say good-bye or at least *au revoir*. If you are remaining for a longer period than a week, the balance of this book will help you enjoy this extra time. But if you have to catch that next plane home, let me say I hope you have enjoyed our one perfect week in San Francisco together.

I know I have enjoyed it! Although I had been many times over to all the places I recommended in this book, I revisited every single one in order to make certain that each day contained the best possible schedule for you. And although it took me many months, not one week, I had you in mind all the time. In parting, I can only hope you will return in the very near future so that we can take up where we must now leave off.

PART TWO

Two- and Three-Day Trips
Around San Francisco

A Two- or Three-Day Trip
Up the Coast to Mendocino

(Recommended between April and October)

O. K. I ADMIT IT—ever since I first set foot in San Francisco over twenty years ago, I have been madly in love with the place. I have spent a great deal of time in nearly every nook and cranny of Europe, circled the Pacific, been just about everywhere. But San Francisco remains my favorite area in the world in which to live. Why? Well, the pace is less hectic than in most major metropolitan areas, yet there is an extraordinary variety of art and entertainment, equal on a per capita basis to any great cultural center. The city's range of exciting dining places is a restaurant-goer's dream come true (for more on this dearest-to-my-heart subject, see "Why is San Francisco Such a Great Restaurant City?"). Its weather is politely moderate but should February's wetness get you down, you can always hop an hour's flight to Palm Springs to bask in the sun or drive only a few hours to the finest ski slopes in the West.

Perhaps most important is that San Francisco doesn't close you in. Its constant around-the-corner views, the consciousness of sky, the briskness of ocean breezes all alleviate the stifling asphalt-jungle aura of New York, or Tokyo, or Milan. And should you desire an even greater respite from steel and concrete, all you need do is drive but a few miles to find yourself in beautiful, unspoiled country, where pine needles crackle underfoot, the surf pounds and the stars are touchable. And this is exactly what we are going to share on our special side trip up the coast.

Almost all guidebooks to the San Francisco area list a visit to Carmel at the top of their "out-of-town" trips. And perhaps I would have done so, too—twenty years ago. But Carmel is fast changing. It has become the shopping mecca for thousands upon thousands of visitors who clog the narrow streets endlessly circling the town's few square blocks in search of that nonexistent parking place. So while I do recommend a visit to Carmel a few pages on, tying it in with a journey down the Big Sur Coast to the Hearst Castle, I believe the ideal change of pace from city life to the open spaces is achieved by heading north to Mendocino.

THE FIRST DAY

8:00 a.m. Whenever I travel, I like to get started early. I like early morning trains, planes, buses, whatever—and that includes driving. It seems to me that if I plan to leave later in the day, I just fritter away the morning hours waiting to go and rechecking to see if I have packed everything. So pack up your rental car and get started.

What to take along? Let's see. You will need only informal wear. The one restaurant which insists upon neckties, I boycott. So take some casual sunny weather togs (it never gets scorching hot, but it can be warm), as well as some more sturdy stuff just in case the fog is in. Our destination —the Little River Inn (707-937-5942)—has a 9-hole golf course, while a few miles away in the midst of the giant redwoods is the Mendocino Tennis Club (for reservations: 707-937-0007). So throw in the appropriate sports gear. And should fishing be your hobby, steelhead and salmon abound here. Nightlife is absent from this rural scene so bring along your dominoes, cards and some good books . . . or just your desire for quietness.

Because of the scenic beauty, I am recommending a leisurely non-freeway route which will take you about 5 hours to travel, not counting any lengthy stops. Therefore, a hearty breakfast might be in order. However, since I have never found an exciting place to lunch along the way to the Little River Inn, you should plan to be there before 2:00 p.m. when its kitchen closes until dinner time.

With the car packed, head out to now familiar Van Ness

Avenue, turn left onto Lombard Street and cross the Golden Gate Bridge. Luckily, you will be going in the opposite direction of the morning-hour commuter traffic. On the Marin County side, continue on up the highway for about 4 miles until you see a sign indicating "Mill Valley, Stinson Beach, Highway 1." Take this turnoff to the right. Highway 1 will bring you right to the front door of the Little River Inn some 150 miles later.

You will remember the first few miles of Highway 1 if you took the Muir Woods outing recommended on the third day's schedule. However, Highway 1 soon becomes filled with twists and turns as it roller-coasters over the foothills to the ocean. From the crests of some of the headlands on a clear day, you can see forever . . . and that includes portions of San Francisco even though you are now in the country. After dipping to sea level at Muir Beach, Highway 1 shoots abruptly upward again and suddenly below you are the sands of Stinson Beach.

The next stretch is along gentle cattle-grazing land and through sleepy little hamlets like Olema and Marshall, where the population figures on the road signs number less than the guest list at a successful city cocktail party. Along Tomales Bay you will see oyster farms, but unfortunately, these oysters are enormous and not particularly appealing.

Highway 1 now cuts inland through more dairy land and through Bodega Bay. In this little town, known for its salmon fleet, Alfred Hitchcock shot his classic "The Birds." Remember when Tippi Hedren was suddenly attacked by that first gull? Well, it was right in the middle of that small harbor on your left. By the way, if you got away late and will not be able to reach Little River (still some 3 hours away) in time for the 2:00 p.m. lunch curfew, you might lunch here at The Tides. The only dish I have enjoyed here is the salmon, but then salmon is *the* fish along this entire route and you will be savoring it superbly prepared at the Little River Inn, so I do hope you love salmon!

Ten miles further at Jenner, Highway 1 crosses a high bridge spanning the mouth of the Russian River; and 13 miles later brings you in sight of Fort Ross. Not too long ago, Highway 1 ran right through this old wooden fort but in order to better preserve this historic spot, the highway now skirts the high stockade. If you wish to visit the fort, you must park in a lot to the left of Highway 1 and take a long walk. If you did not stop at Bodega Bay, this is a great place for a welcome leg-stretch.

Fort Ross was constructed in 1812, when a party of Russians accompanied by native Alaskans landed there. Their purpose in erecting the fort was multiple: to plant wheat for their Alaskan settlements, to hunt for otter, and to trade with the Spanish who owned California but had advanced only as far north as San Francisco. In fact, the Spanish never knew about Fort Ross, until it was too late. And as you can see, the fort's strategic position enabled the Russians to decline all "invitations" to leave. Only a couple of buildings still stand and even they have been restored. In the northeast corner is a chapel, while in the southeast is an octagonal blockhouse with gun emplacements facing the sea, the primary access to the fort until the 1920's.

After leaving Fort Ross, continue on up Highway 1 for about 75 miles to the Little River Inn, our destination. The inn proper, a white Maine-style building dating from 1853, stands on a small rise to the right of the highway, looking out over an inlet and the endless Pacific. Where pioneers once stood watch for arriving sailing vessels which brought long-awaited news from the East and fresh provisions, you now can stand watch for a salmon fleet or perhaps even some migrating gray whales. However, since the time is fast approaching 2:00 p.m., you had better get into the dining room before it is too late.

Not too long ago, the Mendocino Coast around Little River was strictly a haven for fishermen. All they wanted ashore were a decent bed, a well-stocked bar, and wholesome no-nonsense grub. Then this incredibly beautiful coastline was "discovered" by vacationeers and soon, the small town of Mendocino (just about 3 miles further up Highway 1) began to court fancier food, artsy galleries, "shoppes" with cute names, and the inevitable fume-spewing tour buses. Throughout this change, the Little River Inn has stayed pretty much the same. Sure, they added a new wing and cottages, but thankfully they haven't touched their menu or their style. And, to me, it still remains head and shoulders above every place around. You won't find anything from *Larousse Gastronomique* on the menu, but you will enjoy the finest ingredients, superbly prepared in a simple, frill-less fashion.

Take, for example, their clam chowder. Now that is one of the finest Boston clam chowders this side of Beacon Hill. I would gladly trade every vatful of that stuff they dole out at San Francisco's Fisherman's Wharf for just one bowl of this paragon of chowders. Milky white, chock-full of tender clams, and a judicious amount of potato and onion, it is happily free of gelatinous thickeners and other alien intruders like green peppers. Simply sweet and delicious!

The unmistakable co-stars of the Little River's menu are abalone and salmon. In fact, the former is such a knockout favorite that it is available morning, noon and night! Yes, abalone for breakfast at Little River is a decided possibility when you discover how perfectly it is prepared. In case you are not familiar with abalone, let me say that it can be very temperamental. To begin with, the flesh of these rock-clinging mollusks must be cut just right; the pounding to tenderize them must be expertly done; then the filets must be cooked with consummate care, the timing measured in seconds. Even with these precautions, I have found abalone to be the ficklest of creatures, with the texture at times varying from slice to slice on the same plate. However, of all the abalone-expert places I know, the Little River Inn has by far the highest batting average. Oh, yes, and don't be surprised if the luncheon menu lists the abalone as a "sandwich." Actually, it's not a sandwich as the toasted-and-buttered roll slices are served on the side as a garnish.

Salmon requires perhaps only a modicum less culinary talent for its preparation, but the emphasis here is on freshness. And with the salmon fleet in view off the front porch.

that is assured. Also, the Little River Inn's kitchen understands that the preservation of the salmon's sweet moistness is achieved by judicious cooking. Therefore, your order will be broiled just long enough to cook it through, but not to dehydrate it.

What to have for dessert? Berry cobbler, of course! Served piping hot, the ice cream topping melts into creamy rivulets, tantalizing your taste buds with an ideally slight undersweetness. Impeccable clam chowder, award-winning abalone or salmon, and down-home berry cobbler . . . a lunch to cherish in your gastronomic memory bank.

There is no need for me to plan the remainder of your afternoon. You will want to unpack and rest up after that long drive. If it is sunny, you might wish to walk down to the beach at Van Damme State Park adjacent to the inn. Otherwise, just collapse in front of your view of the ocean and relax.

For dinner, there are two places I can recommend—the Little River Inn and the Ledford House. However, your decision cannot be impulsive. In fact, during the height of the summer, dinner reservations in the latter should be made as far in advance as your reservations at the inn. The Ledford House is very small and can sell out a week or two in advance. So plan your dinners for your stay and the minute your plans are finalized, pick up the telephone and make your reservations.

My favorite restaurant in the area outside the Little River Inn is the Ledford House, Highway 1, Little River, (707-937-0282; reservations imperative; located about ½ mile south of the Little River Inn). This little house dates from 1862 and has a close cheery atmosphere which is toasty warm on a foggy, bleak night but somewhat smothering on a warm one. The owner-chef personally prepares every dish, using only fresh ingredients, and often-encountered lengthy waits do little to defeat her considerable talent, which includes a kitchen savvy evident in the limited but inventive menu she prepares. For example, a satiny fresh mushroom-onion soup successfully merges the two distinct flavors, yet allowing neither to relinquish its individuality. The Ledford's salads are usually radiantly garden-fresh lettuce and scallions, topped with a rich cheesy dressing and perhaps a soupcon of sunflower seeds for texture contrast.

During the salmon season, the Ledford House offers up this beautiful fish in two or three different styles, depending on the whim of the chef. You can rest assured that regardless of which mood Ms. Mastin might be in, her salmon will be handsomely prepared. A steak is offered for those diners who must have it, but another meat selection is also on hand. I found the lamb chops with a grated cheese coating exceptional. Accompanying vegetables are always fresh and usually lightly steamed, not boiled. Bravo! Since I am a confirmed chocoholic, I considered the orange liqueur an intrusion into the otherwise beautiful Chocolate Mousse. Coffee was perfection. (Do you think we should hold a San Francisco restaurant-owner convention in Mendocino and show them what coffee is all about?) The wine list invites you to explore the output of some of California's lesser known vintners.

THE SECOND DAY

Since these few days on the Mendocino Coast should be free of all pressures and big city regimens, you will not find me putting together an hour-by-hour activity schedule for you. Just do your own thing. But if you don't mind, I will join you for breakfast, a positively great meal at Little River Inn.

You can start with a brimming glass of freshly squeezed orange juice. Yes, it's not "reconstituted from concentrate" or any of that ersatz orange stuff astronauts supposedly thrive on, but just good ole Mother Nature's orange juice. This usually sets my palate up for a big plate of the inn's Swedish Hotcakes, piping hot and delectably light, accompanied by a few strips of crisp thick-cut bacon. Eggs are done any way you want them—including with abalone! There is plenty of toast, but I cannot resist the freshly baked muffins. Sometimes they are banana, sometimes blueberry, but always superb. The only letdown is the San Francisco style coffee—beige in color, weak in flavor. I wonder if the Ledford House would let me have a doggy bag full of their coffee next time?

Anyhow, with the stick-to-your-ribs lumberjack breakfast under your belt, some type of exercise is called for. So how about heading to the golf course or tennis courts or someplace for a nice walk. The walk I enjoy is a long one: from the inn into Mendocino, then back—a round-trip trek of nearly six miles, but lovely every step of the way. If there are more than two of you, somebody can drive into town and then there is your ride back if you do not feel up to making the to-and-fro walk.

Along this country walk, you will pass grazing fields and old, tumble-down barns seemingly in wait for Andrew Wyeth to come by and capture on canvas the last of their kind. And in mid-summer, the roadside is rife with wild blackberries, just asking to be picked. To me, there is nothing quite like eating these sugar-sweet berries, one by one, while the fresh breeze from the nearby sea fills the earth. And at the end of your hike, there is the quaint little town of Mendocino, perched on a bluff overlooking the Pacific. Here, intermixed with the usual junk shops, are some interesting galleries which invite browsing.

But if the day is soft with sunshine, who can blame you if you just plunk down in a chair or sprawl out on the beach, taking in the sea and the high sky filled with white clouds. At times, I have done just that and perhaps with the distraction of a good book, soon found myself light-years removed from San Francisco and routine. Oh, yes, speaking of light-years. The night sky on the Mendocino Coast is something to experience. So if it is a clear night, on returning from the Ledford House, pull into the parking area at Van Damme State Park. As I said at the beginning of this trip, I have traveled quite a bit and have seen the heavens from ships crossing the Equator and from the edge of the Sahara. But here, the sparkling streams of stars burn with such intensity that you want to reach out and touch them.

THE THIRD DAY

Actually, this day could just as easily be the fourth or the fifth day, depending upon how much time you want to spend in this wonderful area. But eventually, it will be time to start back to San Francisco. And if today is the day for your return, I have some suggestions.

There are three main routes you can take. One is to simply retrace your arrival route back along Highway 1. It certainly is the most scenic and perhaps if you have more than one driver in your party, you might do just that. However, if you wish to make better time, it is best to head inland and meet up with Highway 101. This can be done by either driving about 7½ miles south on Highway 1, then onto Highway 128 for 56 miles of almost unspoiled forests, then onto Highway 101 for about 80 nonstop freeway miles to San Francisco. Or you can drive north through Mendocino and about 9 miles further to Highway 20, which will take you on a 34-mile jaunt through Jackson State Forest to Willits and then to Highway 101. This route is slightly longer than the others (about 28 miles) but it does have one advantage. And that is before turning off onto Highway 20, you can continue 2 miles further north to 356 North Main Street in Fort Bragg. There you will find the Flying Bear, a candy shop that creates the definitive Rocky Road Candy. Equally spectacular are their Chocolate Truffles, Creamy Chocolate Mints, and Belmonts which are a mind-blowing combination of vanilla cream, dark chocolate and crunchy almonds. Naturally, to ward off starvation on the long journey home, I always stop here and load up!

However, man cannot live by Belmonts and Rocky Road alone. And although the Flying Bear chocolates can see you through the restaurant wasteland of Highway 101, sooner or later you must consider dinner. So I will now give you three suggestions which I think might be just right for tonight. All three offer styles of cooking not readily available at Little River; fairly casual attire is perfectly acceptable at all three; and the last two do not accept reservations which means you do not have to arrive at a set time.

Ramona's, 1025 "C" Street, San Rafael (454-0761), is not included in this evening's selections just because it is convenient to your homeward route. Rather, it is recommended as one of the finest Mexican restaurants in the Bay Area. Ramona's is unique not only for the refinement of its south-of-the-border cuisine, but because it is a living extension of the culinary beliefs and personality of a dynamic Mexican lady, the incomparable Ramona herself. Her quicksilver temperament is, for example, reflected in the varied nuances of her offerings—from a surprisingly mild guacamole to the five-alarm heat of the jalapeno chiles topping some of her hors d'oeuvres. And her staunch determination to showcase facets of Mexican cooking other than the ubiquitous Sonora style is clearly evident in dishes such as her masterful Panuchos, a classic from the Yucatan. Here, tender filets of pork rest upon a tortilla base which has been covered with a delicious black bean sauce. And surmounting all are tangy-sweet marinated onion rings.

Another superb dish is the Chile Verde, perfectly trimmed cubes of pork treated to a green chile sauce containing onion, green peppers and pieces of fresh tomato. Ramona's habitues, however, shout their loudest oles over her triumphant Green Enchiladas. And little wonder, with the tender Mexican crepe enveloping an onion and melted-cheese filling, covered with a marvelous green chile sauce, cooled with sour cream. This celestial creation is also offered on a "Gourmet Dinner" which, in addition, boasts a chicken breast bathed in Ramona's intriguing mole sauce, that wild Mexican concoction which numbers chocolate among its vast roster of ingredients! Beer is my beverage with this style of cooking, but none of that vapid American brew. Give me the bold, dark maltiness of a Mexican Noche Bueno to salute the happy world of Mexican cooking and Ramona who brings it to us in such high style.

(To reach Ramona's on your return from Mendocino, simply continue down Highway 101. After entering the San

Rafael city limits you will see on your left the blue-tiled roof of Marin County's Civic Center, designed by Frank Lloyd Wright. Almost immediately thereafter, on your right, is the Lincoln Avenue exit. Take this exit and proceed down Lincoln until you reach the commercial area of town, turning right on Fourth Street to "C" Street, then right to number 1025. On leaving Ramona's, turn right onto Fifth Street; take another right on "B" Street; then left onto Second Street to the freeway entrance to San Francisco.)

Tommaso's, 1042 Kearny Street, San Francisco, (398-9696), is physically located within a tassle's throw of North Beach's topless row; however, its heart and soul lie near Naples. When you first open the heavy front door, you will be greeted by the strong aroma—perfume to me—of an oak fire. Over its glowing coals, Tommaso's bakes their pizzas. But stop! Do not make a mistake you always will regret by saying, "Oh, pizza. I don't want a pizzeria." Tommaso's is not a pizzeria; it just happens to be one of the finest Italian restaurants in town. Yet, because its origins are Neapolitan, it has proudly featured for nearly 50 years that area's specialty—pizza. And this is real pizza, not that cardboard stuff so readily available in drive-ins, dime stores and even movie theaters. Here, at Tommaso's, is the place for you to discover what pizza can and should be.

I usually begin my dinner with two or three salads. Why so many? Well, I never can decide whether I crave the fresh broccoli with olive oil and lemon, or the zucchini in a zesty vinaigrette, or the fantastic sweet peppers. So why be frustrated? I order a selection of them for the table and eat Chinese style! Then, I cannot resist an order of either the Baked Marinated Oysters, piquant with basil, or the Shrimp with Marinara Sauce. Then, and only then, am I ready for my pizza. I will leave your choice of topping up to you. But remember, a truly great pizza is not made of topping alone. Just take a look at the dough—it has a tempting flavor all its own and its edges are light and fluffy. Now, that is pizza!

Of course, you can opt for one of the many other dishes

as your main course. However, here I offer a word of caution. When ordering a pasta, inquire if the kitchen has time to cook yours to order, *al dente*. Tommaso's can become extremely crowded and the pastas, at times, reveal the kitchen's haste by being precooked and even overly so. Soft pasta is a cardinal sin in Italy that can condemn the chef to Dante's lowest level in that big pizza oven down below. So do as the Italians do and make sure your pasta is done right.

For dessert, inquire if the canoli have been refrigerated for long. (By the way, the friendly family at Tommaso's never seems to mind such probing.) If the canoli is fresh, these crispy tubes stuffed with sweetened ricotta are sensational. However, if they have served time in the refrigerator, they can become soggy, losing their most endearing quality. The coffee is suavely Neapolitan and an ideal way to end your evening's visit to bella Napoli. Not to be missed! (If you are driving directly to Tommaso's from Little River, simply take Lombard Street from the Golden Gate Bridge; turn right on Van Ness; then left down Broadway to Kearny Street.)

Grison's, 2100 Van Ness Avenue at Pacific, (673-1888), is that rarest of domestic birds—a truly great steak house. And whenever I wish a respite from unsubtle sauces, flaming fancies and other culinary exotica, I head straight for Grison's. Here, beef is king and reigns supreme. His white-toqued courtiers, visible in the open kitchen, treat him royally. Your preferred cuts—T-bone, New York, filet mignon, club —are all on hand. Their quality is unquestionable and the kitchen's charcoal broiling technique is impeccable, achieving that matchless combination of charred crust and juicy interior.

But Grison's goes much, much further in winning the admiration and loyalty of San Francisco's beef-eaters. First, there is the cole slaw . . . *the* greatest cole slaw anywhere! Freshly shredded, crinkly fresh cabbage tossed with sour cream dressing, it is a must, even if you are not a lover of cole slaw. Then there is the hearty old-fashioned chili beans in individual pots, and baked potatoes that have never suffered entombment in foil. And, would you believe, fresh biscuits with honey? Irresistible! If the finest in steaks and roast beef does not turn you on, then you can try with equal confidence the fresh Calf's Liver or the Fried Spring Chicken. Talk about finger-lickin' good! If Colonel Sanders ever served chicken the likes of this, he would be a five-star general! Grison's is a San Francisco institution and one of the greatest steak houses in America.

A Trip to Yosemite National Park

"YOSEMITE? Oh, I haven't been there in years. I understand it's completely ruined," might be a reaction you encounter if you tell a San Franciscan you are planning a trip there. For years, newspaper accounts of vast overcrowding and of camper caravans belching so much exhaust that the smog blots out the view, have contributed to the popular belief that Yosemite is finished. Well, as once happened to Mark Twain, the reports of Yosemite's death have been greatly exaggerated. Today, El Capitan's "glacier-sculpted face of granite" still looms above the valley floor; sunbeams still "play with spray and mist in rainbow colors" at the base of thundering waterfalls; and when winter's chill leaves the land, the brooks still "sing carols and glees to the spring." Yes, you can still experience these wonders of Yosemite, just as John Muir—the man who wrote the above eloquent words—did many, many years ago.

Mother Nature has not changed but, like everything else, Yosemite has. Today, there are a great many more people in our nation than there were twenty or fifty years ago. And today, there is more leisure time than ever before. So with this greater opportunity for relaxation, more and more people have begun to explore what conservationists and naturalists like John Muir have been writing about for years—the experience of the natural beauties of our world. Therefore, America's system of national parks (one of the greatest assets this country can proudly claim) has become *the* vacationland. And Yosemite is high on the list. In fact, because of its easy access to major metropolitan areas, it has to bear more than its burden of increased interest. Consequently, especially in the peak summer season, there is no doubt that crowds jam the park to bursting. However, the incredible grandeur and drama of Yosemite cannot be eradicated so easily.

My two favorite times of year to visit the park are spring and fall. In the spring, the valley is at its most spectacular, for the falls, fed by the melting snow, are at their fullest and their thunder is an awesome proclamation of the beginning of a new cycle of life. In the fall, the valley is garbed in a more serene air, the leaves are turning, and the squirrels and chipmunks become more brazen as they busily hunt for their winter stores. In the winter, snowstorms can curtail my favorite pastime, hiking; while in the summer, the crowds fence me in.

If you must visit Yosemite in peak season, you can get away from much of the hubbub by taking hikes away from the more populated areas. And believe me, Yosemite's back paths will open up for you a mountain paradise. If you do not want to backpack all the way in, you still will be amazed at how just a quarter-mile further along a secluded trail leads into the quiet beauty of nature. More than likely, you will still meet a few folks along the way, but their friendly, "we are all one," murmured greetings blend with the environment.

In order to enjoy these hikes, you must come prepared. For the lesser hikes, that means with what the British would call "sensible shoes." For more arduous climbs, proper hiking boots and equipment are necessary. Also, if you would like to try your hand (and feet) at more strenuous mountaineering or rock climbing, there is a school located in the valley.

Yosemite's lakes and rivers offer invigorating swimming opportunities, although you might find the warmer waters of the pools at Yosemite Lodge and/or the Ahwahnee Hotel a little more congenial. Seeing the valley by bicycle or horseback is possible; fishing licenses and tackle are available in the village store. For more citified sporting, the grounds of the Ahwahnee has two tennis courts and a putting green; and the Wawona Hotel, an hour's drive from the valley, has a 9-hole course. So after reading this list of possible Yosemite activities, be sure you take with you the appropriate gear. Oh, yes, that reminds me: men should be sure to include in their suitcases a tie and jacket, requirements for admission into the Ahwahnee dining room at night.

As with most national parks, one concessionaire handles all the accommodations. In this case, it is the Yosemite Park and Curry Company. In the valley proper, lodgings are provided to fit any budget. The most economical and understandably Spartan are the canvas tent-cabins at Camp Curry —with the rooms and cabins at Yosemite Lodge slightly more costly. The "de luxe" way of life is evident at the glorious Ahwahnee Hotel, one of my favorite hotels in the U.S. For reservations at any of these locations, call the toll free number (800) 692-5811; out of California, call (209) 372-4671. And make your reservations as far in advance as possible. Yosemite is booked at least one month ahead during the peak season, and almost that far ahead for the rest of the year. I have always found the reservations to be handled with complete efficiency, including a written confirmation.

Thousands of campsites are available in the valley; but as of this writing, they cannot be reserved in advance and are available only on a first-come/first-served basis. That means in the summer months, the "No Campsites Available" sign is hung out very early in the day.

Although I have never pitched a tent in Yosemite in the twenty years I have been regularly visiting the park, I have upgraded myself from a Camp Curry tent to a balconied room at the Ahwahnee. And to be quite candid, it didn't take me long to accomplish this because I fell in love with the Ahwahnee at first sight. It really does not look like a hotel but rather reminds me of some enormous stone and wood hunting lodge built at the base of granite cliffs which arch hundreds of feet above it. And the interior is a haven for those of us who suffer claustrophobia in the cramped Hiltonesque lobbies of today's hotels. The two-storied lounge has a fireplace as spacious as some hotel rooms! And wait until you see the dining room with its vaulted ceiling and enormous windows looking out onto a meadow.

With all this breathing room, the Ahwahnee seems almost impervious to the crowded conditions in the village. Even when the hotel is completely filled, as it invariably is, there is enough quiet space for everyone. Well, more about the Ahwahnee when you arrive in Yosemite. Now, it's time you get going.

THE FIRST DAY

I have devoted as much thought to your departure time for Yosemite as I have to the route you should travel. And you will understand why as you read on. As I have mentioned before, I am of the "early departure" school of travel. However, Yosemite presents a problem. Although the Ahwahnee now posts a check-out time of 11:00 a.m. (certainly an inhospitable change from their more leisurely 2:00 p.m. of a decade ago!), they caution that rooms may not be ready for occupancy until 3:00 p.m. And an even more discouraging sign is posted at the Yosemite Lodge, upping their check-in hour to an unbelievable 6:00 p.m.! Therefore, if you arrive at either the hotel or lodge early in the day, you can find yourself tired from a long drive with nowhere to go except to a lobby chair, to wait and wait.

Also, while San Francisco has long been a restaurant-goer's mecca, once outside its furthest boundary, you find yourself in a gastronomic desert with Denny's and Howard Johnson's as relay posts. So I recommend you enjoy a considerable brunch in the city at Sears', 439 Powell Street, between Post and Sutter, (986-1160), and then set off for Yosemite at . . .

10:30 a.m. Have the desk clerk in your hotel direct you to the nearest on-ramp to the San Francisco-Oakland Bay Bridge. When you have crossed to the East Bay side, follow the signs to Interstate 580, a truck-prohibited stretch which enables you to skirt Oakland. Soon, 580 swings eastward, crossing a range of coastal hills and on into the upper reaches of the mighty San Joaquin Valley. It won't be long before you will see a sign indicating "580 to Interstate 5, Fresno, Los Angeles": take this swing to the right.

As any map will show you in full detail, Yosemite is accessible via three basic routes from the San Francisco area. The seemingly straightest, as-the-crow-flies trek would be the northern course, via Highway 120. Although this route appears to be the shortest, the last stretch is a tortuous, long, narrow mountain road with few turnouts for slow-moving cars. Also, this approach is closed in the winter.

The California Automobile Association recommends the middle route, which would have you leave Interstate 580, taking Highway 132 to Highway 99, then south to Merced where you join Highway 140 through Mariposa to Yosemite Valley. This route is regarded as the quickest (approximately 4½ hours) and it is the one by which you will return to San Francisco after your stay. My perennial path to Yosemite takes about 5 hours, but you can consider the additional half-hour of driving a wise investment that will pay off in a grand "visual" dividend at the end of the drive.

You see, Yosemite Valley is cut lengthwise by the Merced River. Arriving by the two northern routes, you enter the valley by a road which follows the river's north bank, which gives you a gradual awareness of the mammoth cliffs and domes that wall the valley. The southern route, however, passes through the long Wawona tunnel on the more elevated south bank of the river. And on exiting the tunnel, the entire panorama of the valley is suddenly thrust upon you, as though you had just pushed open the doors of a vast cathedral with granite pillars rising thousands of feet above the floor. After having experienced this view dozens of times, I still break into goose bumps whenever I emerge from the Wawona tunnel into Yosemite's valley.

So, if you wish to share this memorable moment, you must continue down Interstate 580, ignoring the "Yosemite, Highway 132" sign, to Interstate 5, California's most super of super-highways. Stretching before you will be a seemingly endless ribbon of concrete, running arrowstraight as far as the eye can see. On your right is the Diablo Mountain Range—not the colossal granite giants you will see keeping watch over Yosemite but rather grass-covered, softly molded hills, often cultivated with fruit trees and vegetable crops. On the left, you will catch view of the gigantic California aqueduct, a 500-mile engineering miracle which carries the run-off from Northern California's mountains to the Los Angeles area. And off in the distance lies the fertile San Joaquin Valley.

Soon, another Yosemite sign will tempt you to Highway 140 but ignore this one, too. The exit you want is Highway 152 East, marked "Los Banos" which, for 42 miles, takes you across the heart of the valley, passing miles of cotton fields, one of California's biggest crops. Highway 152 then merges with southbound Highway 99; 10 miles later, you will exit from 99 to the right, at the sign indicating "Millerton Lake, Yosemite."

Immediately after taking this exit, turn left onto the overpass which carries you to the east side of the freeway. Continue on ahead, crossing the railroad tracks and swinging onto Cleveland Avenue. Proceed along Cleveland for about 1½ miles, then swing right over a small bridge. Immediately after the bridge, turn left onto Highway 145; here, there is a sign indicating the direction to Yosemite. Fourteen miles later, turn left onto Highway 41, now heading north through the Sierra Nevada foothills to the park. Within a few miles, you will notice that the figures on the elevation markers increase as you climb to 5,120 feet to the park's entrance.

2:45 p.m. At the entrance, you will be required to pay an auto permit fee. Be certain to save the receipt since you may be called upon to surrender it when leaving the park. The ranger stationed at the entrance also will hand you a copy of *Yosemite Guide,* a biweekly publication containing a wealth of information about the park and what events may be taking place during your stay. If you do not receive a copy, ask where you may pick one up.

Once in the park, you must make a decision. If you are weary, you will probably want to turn left and proceed straight to your destination, the Ahwahnee Hotel, still 45 minutes away. However, if you have been sharing the driving duties or are not that tired, you may wish to turn right for 2 miles to the Mariposa Grove where the "Big Trees," the redwoods, reach up into the heavens. Not too many years ago, you were allowed to drive right into the grove. Now, with the vast influx of visitors, a parking area has been constructed from which you can walk into the grove or, better yet, take a free hour-long tram ride through the entire grove. From the tram's open carts, you will be able to feel the awesome strength of these redwoods, the largest plants known to man.

Even native Californians, accustomed to seeing these giant redwoods, never fail to be somewhat amazed by them. But the impression they make on first-time viewers is often something to write about . . . just as this beautiful encounter was set into words in the *Yosemite Guide*:

"It was the last stop of the tour of the Mariposa Grove of Giant Sequoias. The evening light was already creating rays of shadows. A small, ancient man ignored the reasonings of his family and left the tram. He carefully selected a spot to sit, and walked slowly and purposely to it. There he viewed the massive, ancient tree for the first time alone. As his family left, his grandson ran down to join the man. Later they would both board the next tram back down to the parking area. But for now, the man studied the tree and thought. Finally, he bowed deeply and got up. 'He has traveled all the way from Japan,' the grandson explained to the ranger now shaking hands with the old man. 'He thanks you for it . . . for taking care of it.' The ranger didn't know Japanese, but obviously was understanding the man quite well."

This little vignette has two messages for me. First, these giant redwoods do require a reverent approach by man in order to absorb into his consciousness what the trees have been, what they are now, and what they will continue to be long after we are gone. And the other message is that they are still here not only because our government comprehends the need of conserving them, but also because there are marvelously devoted men and women—America's park rangers—who take care of them for us, day and night.

If you have taken this tram ride to the "Big Trees," it should now be about 4:00 p.m., time to head for the hotel. Simply drive back to the entrance gate and then proceed on toward Yosemite Village.

As you travel along this lovely road in the park, be careful to keep alert for deer and other animals, especially at this time of day when dusk is near. In the park, you will come across many animals, the most common being chipmunks, squirrels, deer and sometimes bear. Contact with all animals should be avoided for both your sake and their's. First of all, you should not feed any of the animals. Naturalists tell us that while it may seem a kindness to offer food to a foraging fawn or cute little bushy-tailed squirrel, it is bad for them. This kind of pampering results in the animals losing their ability to forage for themselves; and when there are not enough visitors around, those animals spoiled in this fashion may die. My secretary, a staunch natural-food buff, also cringes at the mere thought of these wild animals being exposed to the devitalized chemicals in man's food.

On the other side of the coin, any wild animal can be hazardous to your health. Bears are by far the most dangerous; however, even docile appearing deer have extremely sharp hoofs and smaller animals, such as chipmunks, can be rabid or carry parasites harmful to man. So just watch the animals, and please do it from a distance.

(A note: Along the road, you will spot a sign indicating that you may turn to a certain frequency on your radio in order to receive messages from the park rangers. Do so; it can be very informative.)

Continuing your drive to the Ahwahnee Hotel, you will catch your first glimpse of the valley as you round a curve—but, in a matter of seconds, you are plunged into the darkness of the Wawona Tunnel. You are asked to turn on your lights because this is not a fancy tiled city tunnel but rather just a rough, dark passage blasted through the solid granite face.

Proceed through the tunnel slowly in order to pull into the parking area *immediately* on the right as you exit. And right there is your reward for taking the route I suggested —one of the greatest panoramas on our planet. And at this time of day, the sun is behind you, illuminating the whole spectacle in soft light, ideal for photography. If you are making this visit in the spring, your view will be further enhanced by the lovely Bridalveil Falls, a long slender ribbon of water which, when blown by the wind, billows out across the cliff's face like a sheer veil. Bridalveil Falls will be on the near right. For those interested in identifying the other major domes, falls and rocks, there is an outline map to assist you.

4:00-5:00 p.m.—depending on whether or not you went to Mariposa Grove and how much time you spent there. Although the changing light of the valley view has a mesmerizing effect, it is time to drive on to the hotel. Two urbanizing aspects which have now become part of the park are the use of one-way roads and a wealth of direction signs. With their help, you will have no difficulty locating the Ahwahnee Hotel at the far end of the valley, beyond the village.

Upon your arrival at the hotel, an attendant will see that your luggage is delivered to the front desk while you are registering. He also will park your car, indicating its position on a small map printed on the envelope into which he will place your car keys.

As soon as you get to your room, call the dining room to make dinner reservations. Since the dining room serves non-guests as well, you must request the hour you wish as soon as possible or you may find it booked. After this is done, postpone those unpacking chores until after you've had tea in the Great Lounge. This late afternoon custom

(5:00 to 5:30 p.m.) is a delightful holdover from a more relaxed and gracious era. And it suits the Ahwahnee ideally. Many is the time I have been out hiking for hours only to quicken my pace back to the hotel, knowing that a steaming cup of beautifully brewed tea was awaiting me. And after a long drive, you might find the tea just as rejuvenating before unpacking and dressing for dinner (remember: jacket and tie for gentlemen).

7:30 p.m. Unlike most modern hotels which often appear like a conglomeration of bars and cocktail lounges under one roof, the Ahwahnee has only one real "bar"—and it's a "beaut." It's called the El Dorado Diggings and is located on the mezzanine. You will have to find it yourself since the hotel does little to publicize it and, in fact, sometimes closes it without notice. The decor is strictly circa '49, a street scene right out of *High Noon*. And somehow, its rough Western charm fits into the Ahwahnee's scheme of things.

8:00 p.m. Unfortunately, the most exciting aspect of your dinner at the Ahwahnee will be the loveliness of the dining room itself. Years ago, I wrote that the food here was "far above average for a hotel." Now, I am sad to say it is "barely average." Consequently, I suggest you restrict your ordering to the most basic dishes such as steaks and plain roasts.

It really is a shame that the Ahwahnee's food has deteriorated, because everything else is very pleasurable. A majority of the staff are young employees who appear to have been trained extremely well. And when they do make an occasional faux pas, they are so polite and good natured that it seems insignificant. Would that the kitchen display such an open, honest style!

10:00 p.m. After-dinner coffee, nowhere as expertly prepared as the afternoon tea, is always available in the Great

Lounge. And on some nights, there is dancing in the Indian Room to the left of the entrance.

THE SECOND DAY

8:00 a.m. Surely, you will not wish to sleep much later than this on your first morning in Yosemite. Awaiting you outside your hotel door is one of the world's most beautiful sights. And you do not even have to travel beyond the back lawn of the Ahwahnee's enclosure to sense that special spirit which is Yosemite.

You know, I'll never forget the time I was sitting in the Great Lounge and upon glancing through the French doors, saw a lone nun peacefully sitting at one of the tables on the terrace. The sun, reflecting off the starched white wimple of her habit, radiated a halo effect in the morning light. She was holding her rosary beads, perhaps lost in prayer or simply deep in thought. I had to hold back an impulsive urge to walk over and ask if she thought Heaven would be more beautiful than this . . . for early morning in Yosemite is, indeed, heavenly.

After your stroll around the grounds, you probably will be ready for a more temporal consideration—breakfast. But first stop by the front desk to see if they have any trail maps on hand, and bring along your copy of the *Yosemite Guide*. Breakfast time will double as planning time.

In the morning, the cavernous Ahwahnee dining room completely sheds its mysterious, magical air of evening and dons a freshly scrubbed face, lit by the radiant morning light streaming through the wall of windows. After you have had your first cup of coffee, you can start perusing the maps and guide to decide what you would like to do today. Let me help.

A great deal of what you do and when you do it depends on: the length of your stay in Yosemite, your hiking ability, and the weather. Let's rule out the latter and assume the day is bright and sunny with only the usual few scattered Sierra clouds. The next consideration is just how much you like to hike or walk. In the valley, there are all kinds of walks—some with no inclines to tax your wind, others requiring fairly good stamina. Then, too, you should consider the length of your stay. As with sightseeing anywhere, be it in a complex of urban museums or in this cathedral of natural wonders, you simply cannot experience everything at once. Pacing your activities is essential for full enjoyment of them. With this in mind, I will recommend three walks.

One walk is to Mirror Lake. The entire walk is along a level paved road (or parallel path) without traffic. It is a little more than a mile in each direction, although you can make the return by shuttle bus.

And here, I would like to say a few words about the shuttle buses in use at Yosemite. Don't be turned off by them. Frankly, they are ideal for Yosemite and probably have contributed greatly in preserving the beauty of the park. You see, a few years ago, traffic in the park was becoming impossible with cars and campers turning every narrow road into a huge traffic jam. The park authorities faced with this problem wisely decided that instead of widening the roads and building more parking lots, thereby destroying huge areas of natural forests and meadows, they would offer visitors an easier means of access—shuttle buses. To encourage the use of these shuttles, many of the existing roads were torn up or narrowed, and then restricted to "shuttles only." The shuttle service goes just about everywhere in the park, with the village as the main transfer point. And it is all free of charge!

Now, to take your walk to Mirror Lake, simply cut across the back lawn of the Ahwahnee to the tennis court; exit through the gate there, turning left on the narrow paved road. Your destination, Mirror Lake, is aptly named since Mt. Watkins is reflected in its waters in a perfect double image.

A second walk (which is a bit more arduous) is a path to the base of Yosemite Falls. To take this walk, exit through the main automobile gate of the hotel. Soon, on the right, you will see a trail marker indicating that Yosemite Falls is a little over a mile away. The trail quickly climbs a bit as it skirts the small hospital and then the village. From this higher vantage point, there are some lovely views of the valley frequently filled with morning mist. Not so lovely, though, are the oft-appearing smog and campfire smoke which dull the view. However, it is an extremely pleasant walk and the reward at the end is Yosemite Falls, one of the most famous falls in the world. From here, you can take a shuttle back to the hotel.

My favorite hike (not walk) is to Vernal Falls. Take the shuttle from the Ahwahnee to the village and then transfer to a shuttle to Happy Isles, the starting point of the hike. Here, the wide and semi-paved trail starts upward, tracing the course of the Merced River on your right. As you hike higher, the sounds of the river cascading over the huge boulders become louder and louder. You will come to a bridge and from here, you will see Vernal Falls about three-quarters of a mile further up river. This is a good resting spot to consider whether you wish to go further or return to the valley floor.

If you do not want to hike much further, I do urge you to at least take the next quarter-mile hike to a lookout of Vernal Falls, clearly marked. Here, from the flat surface of an enormous granite boulder, you seem to be far closer to the falls than the very short distance you covered. It is a dream spot for photographs of those rainbows the sunbeams create in the falls' spray.

If you are ready and able for a further climb, I recommend you veer off this trail to the right at the sign marked "Nevada Falls." The sign indicates a distance of 2.4 miles, but I usually follow the trail only about 1.9 miles to a footpath marked "Yosemite Valley via Misty Trail," which leads back to the valley eventually. This higher climb reveals a fabulous look at Nevada Falls over which the Merced River plunges before coursing to Vernal Falls. And the footpath actually crosses right over the top of Vernal Falls from where you can watch the river close-up as it leaps over the sheer edge. Misty Trail then becomes a down staircase of sorts, cut into the rock face. If the falls are at their height, you will soon understand the significance of the name, Misty Trail.

Of course, you can go further afield either by car or bus transportation. For example, the bus will take you around the Mariposa Grove (if you failed to stop there on the way in) and to Glacier Point. Glacier Point is the 7,214-foot summit you see directly across the Ahwahnee grounds. It surely must be the spot where Whoever created Yosemite sat in satisfaction at His handiwork. You can also climb there by a rather steep 4-mile trail. But whether it is on wheels, horseback, or foot, the view from Glacier Point should be experienced.

Now, it is time you started. Remember to dress appropriately and wear the right kind of shoes. Also, if you will be gone for some time, the hotel has box lunches available which usually must be ordered the night before.

And speaking of lunch, if you do not return to the hotel, you might wish to lunch at Degnan's in the village—decent hamburgers, excellent French fries and salads. Also, in the same building housing Degnan's, there is a well-stocked delicatessen which you may wish to raid for picnic provisions. In any case, have a good day.

4:00 p.m. By now you have probably returned to the hotel, your feet and legs aching with the strain of the walks, but your eyes and soul filled with sights which will remain in your memory for years to come. A dip in the Ahwahnee pool might be nice—then tea, of course.

8:00 p.m. Years ago, I used to look forward to donning jacket and tie after being in boots and hiking shorts all day, and walking into the Ahwahnee's beautiful dining room which seemed to be filled with a grand and festive air. But that was when the cuisine at least approached the elegance of dress. Now, I find I am often annoyed that I have to dress while the kitchen can "rough it." Therefore, when I am especially irked at this sham, I often retreat to Degnan's Loft for dinner. It's not that the food is generally much better here; it's just that in the Loft's extremely informal atmosphere, "average" cooking is easier to tolerate. And, at times, some of Degnan's offerings are far above the Ahwahnee "average"—something which I find strange because both are operated by the same firm! In any event, at Degnan's, I have found a delightful spinach and bean sprout salad, a more than adequate roast beef, and acceptable apple pie.

YOUR SECOND, THIRD OR FOURTH DAY

Yosemite would take months to fully experience. You would have to, for example, wait for the snows of winter to witness an entirely different but still poetic Yosemite. So now I will leave you on your own . . . perhaps to discover on a moonlit night while walking through the meadow adjacent to the hotel, the sheer face of Half Dome bathed in a luminiscent blue, the likes of which you may never see again . . . or perhaps to learn about the whole world of bird life at home in Yosemite from a knowledgeable ranger on a 7:00 a.m. nature walk . . . or maybe to realize that a chair on the terrace looking up at the grey ancient face of Glacier Point is what relaxation is all about.

However, since I have delivered you to this Eden, I will help you find your way back to San Francisco. When you are ready to go (or find you must go), follow the signs indicating "Exits": Highway 140 is the one you will want. From the valley, it will take you out the El Portal Entrance, through the town of Mariposa, and down to the table-top flatness of the San Joaquin Valley, passing enormous turkey farms and peach orchards. At Merced, pick up Highway 99 North, turning off 99 some 37 miles later onto Highway 132 West, which connects up with 580, which will take you right to the Bay Bridge.

After passing through the Treasure Island Tunnel with

the San Francisco skyline now directly ahead, I often think of which view I love the most—the skyline of my home city, one of the most beautiful in the world, or Yosemite from the Wawona Tunnel. And I always end up saying, as you may now feel: "Each is unique. Each I love equally."

But, when it comes to dining out, there is only one city in my mind—San Francisco. And the two recommendations for this evening are both superb restaurants, though dissimilar in style and execution.

Vanessi's, 498 Broadway at Kearny, (421-0890), is a venerable San Francisco dining institution which reportedly first saw light as a legitimate front for a not-so-legitimate backroom card parlor. Today, Vanessi's is readily acknowledged as one of the city's great restaurants—not great in its ambience, mind you, but great in its food. At the bustling open counter, you will find colorful street and night people; in the dark recesses of the bar, middle-aged swingers drown out the vibrant strains of a Hungarian cymbalom; while in the rear dining room, business tycoons find an only somewhat less frantic refuge. What this diverse cross section of localites all share, however, is an enormous respect for Vanessi's Italian-accented cooking.

The menu is very long but it is almost impossible to go astray. Even so, I will point out some perennial favorites. For starters, I consider the Tortellini Veneziana just about the best in town. Here, those little ringlets of pasta (which, according to legend, were modeled after the navel of an ancient chef's comely lady love) are stuffed with meat and blanketed in a supreme cheese sauce, turned blushing pink with tomato. The Linguine with Clam Sauce is another staunch champion—pasta bathed only in the liquid produced by simply sauteeing tiny clams in oil with garlic and herbs. Of course, in ordering these pastas, request they be cooked to order, *al dente*. Also stellar are Vanessi's two versions of Cannelloni, one stuffed with a subtle chicken mixture, the other with a heartier minced beef and spinach.

As for soups, Vanessi's Minestrone is classic; and their Maritata, the marriage soup traditionally fed bridegrooms to fortify them for their wedding night, is a dreamy blend of chicken broth, eggs, cream, cheese and fine pasta.

If the barely passable Yosemite cuisine causes you to lust for a steak in the grand manner, the Culotte Steak on Vanessi's menu is regarded as one of the finest in town. It is also available in a half-order cut, which enables you to enjoy the best of both the beef and pasta worlds! Vanessi's Calf's Liver Steak and veal dishes are worth your attention, too. For dessert, a velvety Zabaione followed by an ebony espresso will reassure you that you are back in gastronomic heaven—San Francisco.

Canlis', Fairmont Hotel, California and Mason Streets, (392-0113), is not a native San Francisco restaurant but rather an import, a member of the renowned Canlis' quartet (Seattle, Portland and Honolulu hosting the others). Perhaps because of this, some chauvinistic San Franciscans tend to dismiss it. I don't and you shouldn't! Canlis' possesses in abundance all the requisites of a truly fine restaurant— handsomely stylish yet unobtrusive decor; delightful, kimono-clad Japanese waitresses who are peerless in efficiency, hospitality and charm; and a solid menu which focuses primarily on expert charcoal broiling. But do not think this last attribute will restrict you solely to a steak dinner. Some of my most cherished Canlis' creations are from the sea rather than the wide open spaces. Take, for example, their captivating Quilcene Oysters. Although listed on the menu as a main course, you can request an appetizer serving—and I urge you to do so. These precious beauties from Washington state waters are lightly pan-fried and set to rest upon a crinkly bed of straw potatoes. One of my favorite appetizers in town! Other aquatic first courses are the excellent Herring in Sour Cream and Salad with Tiny Bay Shrimp. An intriguing salad of Lebanese origin is the Tabuli—fingers of crisp romaine filled with a crunchy melange of minced vegetables and grains with a hint of mint, all in a lemony dressing.

For main courses, anything and everything that can be charcoal broiled is on hand: calf's liver, fresh salmon in season, fresh trout, chicken, and the whole repertory of steaks. Yet, one great Canlis' dish I crave, especially on a warm night, never even gets close to a flame—the Steak Tartare. This rendition is totally unlike any I have experienced elsewhere, except at another Canlis'. In fact, I consider it more of a raw-beef salad. Here, the seasoned, finely ground beef is molded into a flat loaf, topped with first a layer of minced onion, then a tier of minced tomato, and then capped with green olives and capers. A marvelously refreshing variation of a classic! For dessert: fresh strawberries in a surprisingly good replica of Devon cream. While Canlis' may not have been born in San Francisco, it certainly has earned its culinary pedigree.

A Three-Day Trip to Carmel, Monterey, Big Sur and San Simeon

ALMOST EVERY VISITOR to San Francisco has heard about Carmel and wants to see it. I think some knowledge about Carmel-by-the-Sea is important, however, before you decide to include this side trip in your stay.

If the person who told you about Carmel visited there fifteen or twenty years ago, his or her experience would be somewhat different today. Carmel initially achieved its fame by being the epitome of the sleepy seaside hamlet, replete with a rather quaint artsy-craftsy character. And it still valiantly strives to maintain its village aura by eschewing streetlights and house numbers. Many of the houses are constructed in picturesque styles which smack of the kind of architecture usually reserved for illustrations in children's books. With this storyland ambience, it is easy to understand why a Carmel stay was once considered the ideal balm to soothe the psyche, traumatized by modern urban hurly-burly.

As word got around, however, hordes of city folk the world over wanted to partake of the Carmel elixir and in so doing, they changed many of the very qualities they sought. In their frantic rush to escape big-city commercialism and pressure, they created a type of countrified commercialism. During the height of the summer season, Carmel's traffic jams rival in intensity the most clogged city streets. (Traffic ordinances are strict and tightly enforced.) And the once easy-going shop owners who had always welcomed visitors with a smile and had time for a chat, have now taken on a sterner, business-only mien. This also sadly reflects an ideological schizophrenia which seems to infect much of the town. While many Carmelites treat the influx of tourists with disdain and even hostility at times, they cannot survive without the passengers of those thousands of cars which cramp their streets.

Carmel has therefore evolved from the idyllic little village-by-the-sea, into a handsome shopper's mecca, complete with all the problems of overcrowding and commercialism which come hand-in-hand with that kind of "success." And while you still won't find any neon signs on Ocean Avenue or house numbers on the quaint cottages, you will find the latest in international haute-couturier creations, costly antiques, and acres of art. Because I am not enamored with shopping per se, Carmel in this role holds little interest for me.

But . . . Carmel happens to be situated in the heart of one of the most scenically spectacular parts of California, if not the entire United States. And fitted into a three-day trip filled with unrivaled outdoor recreational opportunities, superb dining, some California history, and the majesty of the most awesome meeting of sea and land in the world, Carmel, in this perspective, with its bevy of smart shops and galleries, is a "must-see."

THE FIRST DAY

With ten championship golf courses (both public and private) and over a dozen tennis clubs (mostly public) in the Carmel-Monterey area, the requisite sports equipment is your first packing consideration. You will also want to take along some comfortable shoes for your shopping forays and for climbing over the more than 300 steps at Hearst's Castle. While Carmel is "country casual" tweedy in dress, men will want to pack a tie for dining in a superb French restaurant. The entire area is renowned for its benignly pleasant (although, at times, foggy) climate. So pack accordingly and if you forget to pack something, you can always buy it in Carmel—no matter what "it" may be!

10:00 a.m. After a fine breakfast at Sear's, Mama's, the Stage Delicatessen or in your hotel, start off by locating the nearest on-ramp to Highway 101, south to Los Angeles. The most direct route to our destination is to remain on Highway 101 for about 90 miles before turning off onto Highway 156 for the Monterey Peninsula. Doing so, however, presents an unattractive landscape, tracing the Bay's western perimeter through dull industrial areas for the first 50 some miles. Since this stretch is also the primary commercial avenue to and from San Francisco, and passes the airport, the traffic can be fairly heavy.

Therefore, I suggest that once on 101 South, you watch for a sign indicating "Highway 280, Daly City" which will appear in a couple of miles. Take this turnoff to the right and continue on 280, following the many signs to San Jose. You will first cut through the southern residential portion of San Francisco, then sweep gently up through the hillside bedroom communities of San Mateo County, overlooking the Bay. Soon you will be viewing some lovely hillscapes, with the waters of the Crystal Springs Reservoir glimmering in the sun. Then on through the horse-loving community of Woodside, skirting behind Stanford University and connecting up with 101 again just south of San Jose.

Now follow the signs indicating "Highway 101, Los Angeles." This drive takes you through rich farmlands, past prune orchards and grape fields, increasingly threatened by the encroachment of suburban sprawl. Forty-nine miles later, take the turnoff to Highway 156, marked "Monterey Peninsula." Suddenly, you will find yourself in the "Artichoke Capital of the World" with acres upon acres of the thistle-like plants stretching to the horizon. Highway 156 then swings into Highway 1 South, which will be the main artery of your travels for the next three days.

Remain on Highway 1 as it by-passes Monterey and do not take any of the Carmel exits. Our destination, the Tickle Pink Motor Inn, is not in Carmel proper but in Carmel Highlands, 4 miles south of Carmel. Watch for a sign on the left indicating the Highlands Inn; then 800 feet later, turn left into its rising driveway, which is marked "Highlands Drive." Continue on up the drive, passing through the Highlands Inn's parking lot onto the Tickle Pink, right next door.

For over fifteen years, the Tickle Pink Motor Inn, P. O. Box 3276, Carmel, CA 93921, (408) 624-1244, has been my most favored place to stay while visiting the Carmel-Monterey area. First of all, it perches on a cliffside overlooking the Pacific Ocean, an important advantage over almost all Carmel proper hotels and motels. Each and every room—from the most modest to the lovely suites with functioning stone fireplaces—shares this view. And almost every room has a balcony overlooking the sea, where visitors can savor their morning continental breakfast, presented with the compliments of the inn.

Secondly, I enjoy being removed from the cloyingly "cute" atmosphere of many "downtown" Carmel inns, which make feeble attempts at re-creating English manors and the like. The Tickle Pink is an extremely comfortable, modern motor inn—there is no need for it to try to be something that it isn't. And lastly, in a day and age when housekeeping in tourist-oriented hotels and motels is becoming shockingly poor, the Tickle Pink is scrupulously clean. Had I not known better, I would have sworn I was the first occupant ever on my last stay.

Of course, I am not the only traveler who knows of and swears by the Tickle Pink and its enviable charms and comforts. You will, therefore, have to reserve as far in advance as possible. The room charge is somewhat more than the usual run-of-the-mill motel. If you wish to splurge a bit more, ask about their spacious suites, especially the two on the top level. To me, they are worth every cent.

Since the drive down from San Francisco takes anywhere from 2½ to 3 hours, it should now be approaching 1:00 p.m. If you are hungry and would like a bite before starting out on your afternoon or, if for some reason your room is not ready, stroll over to the adjacent Highlands Inn. Otherwise, if your breakfast was sufficient, you might wish to wait until dinner.

2:00 p.m. Settled into your Tickle Pink room, it is now time to put your priorities in order—Mother Nature or shopping. If you wish to experience, at close hand, that marvelous meeting of land and sea visible through your picture windows, all you need do is drive about 2 miles back up Highway 1 (toward Carmel) and pull into the Point Lobos State Reserve. Regarded by many as one of the most beautiful pieces of California coast, this 1,500-acre park boasts a 6-mile shoreline, along which you can hike and explore the incredible world of tide pools. During low tide, these pools are exposed and in them are microcosms of life—starfish, hermit crabs, sea urchins and sea anemones. Squatting by one of the pools and witnessing the beauty within, can mesmerize me for hours.

If, however, you are more enchanted at the moment by man's creations in fashions, art, jewelry, etc., then drive another mile or so beyond Point Lobos to the Ocean Avenue turnoff to the left, which will take you right into the heart of Carmel. Here, you will not require my guidance. What you will need are good walking shoes and a deck of credit cards. Oh, yes, you will also need to find a parking space. If you skipped lunch and are now regretting it, walk over to Patisserie Boissiere on Mission Street, between Ocean and 7th, for tea or coffee and a piece of fabulous French pastry.

5:30 p.m. Time to think about returning to the Tickle Pink and enjoying the late afternoon sun over the sparkling Pacific. (If you are in Carmel and wish to take back some cocktail fixings with you, stop in at the superb Mediterranean Market at Ocean and Mission Streets. If you do not want to bother, you can always enjoy the same view from the cocktail lounge at the Highlands Inn next door and leave the mixing to them.)

7:30 p.m. Time to head north again, but this time for dinner. Armed with an advance reservation (as usual, I am assuming you have read ahead and have made the necessary telephone call) and with the men in the party dressed in ties (not demanded, but appreciated), head back up Highway 1 toward Carmel. Turn left down Ocean Avenue to Mission, then right for approximately 3 blocks—L'Escargot is on Mission near Fourth, Carmel, (408) 624-4914.

L'Escargot is perhaps the most accurate replica of a true French country restaurant in all California. Whereas other "auberges" and "bistrots" often capture the simplicity of authentic French country-inn decor, shun hard liquors, and have a way of duplicating the cheery yet uniquely French reserve in ambience, I know of no other which completely reproduces the correct style of menu, cuisine and service. L'Escargot's menu is wisely limited yet sufficiently varied— I could dine for several nights in a row without being bored. The French touch is even more evident in the style in which the dishes are presented without any artificial pomp and completely devoid of those plate garnishes which only detract from the glory of the center attraction.

Let's investigate the dishes themselves. For first courses, four are offered, and, to the best of my recollection, they have remained unchanged for the ten years I have been dining there. But who could ever tire of the scintillating flavor of a real, homemade tomato soup, filled with minuscule pieces of crunchy vegetables. Or who would not be impressed by the pristine quality of the salmon, smoked by the owner, M. Nopert, because he cannot discover commercial ones to please him. The celery hearts in an impressive vinaigrette are impeccable; and the restaurant's namesake, the escargots, are simply the finest I have encountered in the West!

The main course "par excellence" is the Chicken with Cream and Truffles. Nowhere in America (including in New York's most ultra-snobbish and expensive French restaurants) have I uncovered such perfection. The quality of the succulent chicken, its expert golden coat, the ambrosial cream sauce jetted with truffles—all proclaim a mind and heart totally in tune and trained in the art of French cooking.

If you wish a less elaborate dish (it is a misconception

that all French dishes must be sauced), try the plain (!) roast chicken. I can recall once having its equal, many years ago, in a tiny auberge near the forest of Fountaine-bleau. Also, inquire of M. Nopert if there is a fish dish that evening unlisted on the menu. Like a true French patron, Yves Nopert (who happens to be Belgian) cannot resist a fine, fresh fish if he spots one in the morning market. His Chocolate Mousse should be placed on the culinary endan-gered species list, because it is one of the last examples of that sinfully tempting dessert, made of deep, dark, rich chocolate. The wine list is vast, ranging from exalted vintages to some far less costly "finds" unearthed during Nopert's European travels. L'Escargot is one of the great French restaurants in the state and without peer for authentic French country cooking.

10:30 p.m. Before you return to the Tickle Pink, you might wish to stroll along the now nearly deserted streets of Carmel. In the vicinity of L'Escargot, watch your step; Carmel still shuns the urban conveniences of paved side-walks and curbs. Along Ocean Avenue, though, your eyes can focus on the shop windows without distraction. You might relish an after-dinner brandy at the bar in the Pine Inn on Ocean Avenue before heading back down Highway 1 to a sleep, softly lulled by the sound of the ocean surf.

THE SECOND DAY

8:00 a.m. This is the earliest hour at which you can re-ceive your complimentary continental breakfast at the Tickle Pink. You may have to forgo it if golf is your game and you want to get out early. If golf is not your game, it cer-tainly is *the* game of the Carmel-Monterey Peninsula which. sports the title "Golf Capital of the World." You may never have held a putter in your hands, but it is almost certain you have seen photos of the incredible 16th hole at Cypress Point, 220 yards of blue Pacific between tee and green. Tennis is another favored recreation here and the area is dotted with courts. To ensure either golf or tennis availability, it is best to check with your travel agent or golf and tennis clubs at home.

If you do not wish to spend this morning on the greens or the courts, I have a few suggestions. If you spent yesterday afternoon at Point Lobos, perhaps you are ready to poke around Carmel's shops this morning. Or, you might take a journey back in time to the beginnings of Carmel by visiting the mission officially known as the Basilica San Carlos Borromeo del Rio Carmelo. To reach this historic link with California's past and the final resting place of Father Junipero Serra, the founder of California's chain of missions, drive north toward Carmel, taking the Rio Road turnoff to the left. Or, you might wish to just beachcomb along the sandy Carmel beach, depending on what the fog is doing. If you do go, take your camera along to capture the photogenic wind-tortured cypress trees.

About now, you should give some consideration to where or rather, how you wish to lunch. As usual, I have a couple recommendations. The first is a picnic along the north shore of the famed 17-Mile Drive; the second, a fine garden restaurant in the neighboring city of Monterey, where you should spend the afternoon. Whatever your choice, start off by heading back to Ocean Avenue in Carmel.

11:00 a.m. Drive down Ocean Avenue. (If you opted for the picnic, purchase whatever provisions you desire at the Mediterranean Market. And don't forget some pastries from Patisserie Boissiere.) Proceed down Ocean Avenue until you just about reach the beach, turning right at the "17-Mile Drive" sign. Pass through the gate (a $4.00 per auto charge for non-residents); ask for a map; and take the first left, marked "Del Monte Lodge." Then pick up the red-dotted center line which will mark your course throughout the drive.

Actually, you will only be traversing about half of the entire 17 miles, but it is by far the most scenic half. Within minutes, the famed Pebble Beach Golf Links will be on your left. Ranked in the top 10, this course serves as the home of the Bing Crosby Pro-Am Tournament each January. Then you will cut through an exclusive colony of mansions, erected in every imaginable style from Moorish to Modern to Colonial, yet they all have one thing in common—great wealth. Out on a wind-swept point you will view "Lone Cypress," possibly the most painted and photographed tree in all America. Then comes the Cypress Point Club (private) and Fanshell Beach, a crescent of white sand where you can enjoy your picnic. Just a little further on (an ideal after-lunch walk), you will come upon Seal and Bird Rocks, the habitat of shore birds, sea lions and sea otters.

Continuing on the 17-Mile Drive, watch for the sign marked "Pacific Grove Gate" and turn left. The 17-Mile Drive now becomes an ordinary city street. If the time of your visit happens to be in October or early November, I urge you to turn left here onto Lighthouse Avenue and follow the signs to "Butterfly Trees." This six-acre grove is the winter home of the monarch butterflies; enormous clusters of them are best visible in the afternoon sun. Otherwise, turn right and you will soon find yourself in the heart of Pacific Grove, a delightfully Victorian seaside town, founded by the Methodists over 100 years ago as a site for camp meetings.

Whether you turned right or left, everyone must now proceed down Lighthouse Avenue to David, then left downhill to famed Cannery Row. Though immortalized by John Steinbeck as "a poem, a stink, a grating noise," today those attributes have all but vanished. Almost all the ancient, weather-worn canneries have been converted into modern warrens of shops, restaurants, art galleries, etc. Tourists pack them as tightly as their previous occupants—the sardines! At the top floor of number 585, you might make note of Chez Felix, our restaurant selection for later tonight.

Down Cannery Row, hugging the waterfront, you come to Foam Street; turn left, watching for a sign leading to "Pacific Street." Take this exit to the right and proceed down Pacific, and then left onto Franklin; in a few blocks, turn right onto Washington which soon becomes Abrego. On your left, at number 565, a towering clock marks the luncheon restaurant for those who preferred not to picnic. Locate a parking spot nearby. Even if you are not planning to lunch here, this is a good place from which to begin a walking tour of Old Monterey, the former capital of California and one of the most historic cities in the state. But first, a bit about The Clock Garden, 565 Abrego, Monterey, (408) 375-6100, for those who will now enter its gates.

Lunching in the garden of The Clock is like dining in an outdoor nursery in riotous full bloom. The brick patio is alive with potted flowering geraniums and daisies and the thick, plank tables also support pots of growing plants. If consummate care has been lavished in providing a delightfully relaxed, sunny atmosphere, the same infinite attention has been paid to the short yet refreshingly simple menu. Superb homemade soups can act as the opening course or the main attraction, chaperoned by bread and a mini salad. Only one soup is featured each day, but you can bank on its unerring excellence, be it the delicious Clam Chowder or the velvety, egg-thickened Greek Lemon.

The Garden Salad—almost an entire head of crisp lettuce, topped with a wealth of ham, turkey, cheese and countless other goodies—is barely contained in its enormous bowl. The toothsome dressing is thoughtfully served on the side so diners can employ their own discretion in its application. For hot dishes, the Crepes Carlotta are sure-fire winners. After the moist cardboard "crepes" of franchised creperies, it is rewarding indeed to come across real, truly flavorful crepes, golden and rich. A haunting mixture of spinach, turkey and cheese, heightened by a touch of what I believe is cumin, is enveloped within them. Totally delightful! If salmon is in season, the Cold Poached Salmon is faultless in both quality and execution, partnered by a dilled Cucumber Salad. Sandwiches are heartily abundant and the Pecan Pie is my dessert choice. By looking around you at the people who crowd inside the charming garden, you can plainly see that The Clock Garden is not just another "tourist res-

taurant," but one that local residents cherish, just as I do
and, I daresay, you will.

Whether or not you lunched at The Clock Garden, it is
a fine spot from which to begin a small walking tour of Old
Monterey. (The visitor's free weekly newspaper, *Monterey
Peninsula Review,* usually prints the route of a historic
walking tour in each issue which you can use as a handy
guide.) You can start out by turning right as you exit The
Clock's gate, keeping an eye on the dark red stripe on the
roadbed. In about a block, you will pass Estrada Adobe and
then the Stevenson House, home of Robert Louis Stevenson
which contains a collection of memorabilia dating to 1879.
Local Stevenson scholars like to point out that the geography
of Point Lobos is remarkably similar to that of Stevenson's
fictional *Treasure Island.*

Later along the walk you will come upon the Larkin
House, a perfect example of the "Monterey style" of architecture which had its beginnings as Spanish adobe (early
1800's) but was later modified by the New England seamen
with the addition of a second story and a balcony. Colton
Hall on Pacific Street, built in 1847-49, is possibly the
finest of the remaining old buildings. Other interesting structures along the route are the Custom House, the oldest
government building on the Pacific Coast; and California's
First Theater (1846-1847) with its display of theatrical
souvenirs from the past.

How much time you spend viewing and visiting these
historic buildings depends upon your interest and perhaps
the weather. If it is a fine sunny day, this walk is an extremely pleasant way to assimilate some history while enjoying the sun. When you have soaked up enough of both,
simply find your way back to Abrego Street and your car.
To return to the Tickle Pink, continue out Abrego, which
merges into Munras, which brings you right to Highway 1
South.

6:00 p.m. Your last night in Carmel might start out with
cocktails again on your Tickle Pink deck, or you might

decide to drive to Cannery Row an hour or so before your reservation time at Chez Felix and enjoy a relaxed pre-dinner drink at one of the waterside spots. (Warning: Parking meters on Cannery Row are in force until 10:00 p.m.!)

To reach Cannery Row, head up Highway 1 past Carmel, turning off onto Highway 68, marked "Pacific Grove." Continue on 68 as it takes you through a portion of the Del Monte Forest. As you emerge, turn right down Prescott Street directly to Cannery Row at the base of the hill.

8:30 p.m. Chez Felix, 585 Cannery Row, Monterey (408) 373-0556, is an oasis of good cooking in what is basically the "steak-and-lobster tails" culinary wasteland of Cannery Row. Here, from an upstairs vantage point, you can look out over the street and onto the bay beyond while enjoying extremely well-prepared French cuisine with a zesty Provencale accent. The Onion Soup is not the bitter, dark brew you find in all too many American French restaurants, but rather a handsomely sweet stock, simmering gently under its crusted cheese lid. The Crab Bisque is more forthrightly robust in character than most bisques, and its flavor is given even more spunk by an offering of rouille, that fiery southern France concoction of garlic, peppers and olive oil which should be placed atop floating toast rounds.

For main courses, Chez Felix's presentations are less "pure" in the French manner than those of L'Escargot since they are amply garnished with fresh vegetables, rice, etc., but they are beautifully prepared. My favorites are the Scampis Carmarguaise, *fresh* Monterey Bay prawns treated to a touch of garlic; and the Sweetbreads enveloped in a thick, luxuriant mushroom sauce. The Chocolate Mousse contains a distinctive addition of chestnut puree. All in all, fine French cooking at moderate prices—an unusual and welcomed combination in this day and age.

10:00 p.m. After dinner, you may enjoy strolling along Cannery Row and dropping into one of the local places for a nightcap, or simply retracing your drive back to the

Tickle Pink and enjoying a final drink at the bar in the adjacent Highlands Inn.

THE THIRD DAY

Your last chance to get in a morning of golf or tennis, or to make up your mind if that seascape painting you spotted in that Carmel side-street gallery would really suit the den wall. Then, it is packing and setting off down the coast.

Perhaps on your numerous treks back and forth from Carmel and Monterey to the Tickle Pink, you may have noticed a rather ominous sign on the roadside heading south reading: "Curves and hills next 74 miles." To those unaccustomed to California's coastal terrain, I want to impress upon you just what that means. It means that Highway 1, your approach to Hearst's Castle at San Simeon, will be at most times a two-lane roller coaster, clinging precariously to the sheer sides of the Santa Lucia Mountains with only a few feet of gravel and perhaps a low stone wall between you and the Pacific Ocean a couple hundred feet below. Even though I have covered this stretch many times, I would *not* traverse it in fog, rain or dark of night. I certainly do not want to frighten you out of this important leg of your trip because the rewards in unique scenery and Hearst's Castle are well worth the effort. But you should be aware of what lies ahead.

11:00 a.m. All packed, you now exit from the Tickle Pink, turning left onto Highway 1. Our lunch destination (about 25 miles south) can be reached in 40 minutes, so you have plenty of time to take it easy, pulling onto some of the numerous turnouts on the right to better contemplate the vast panorama. Words fail to accurately describe this powerful meeting of land mass and surging sea—a symphony in itself which is called Big Sur Country.

12:00 noon By this time, you should be at Nepenthe, (408) 667-2345, where you will be having lunch. Aptly named after the mythical drug which possessed the magical power to induce forgetfulness of sorrow, Nepenthe is far more than just a place to eat—it is a state of mind. The moment I arrive, my mind immediately casts off "city concerns" and begins to quietly flow with the sweep of the mountains that curve into the sea. Here, 800 feet above the Pacific, you are in another world, one without hassles, one that is an extension of nature. The restaurant (I hate to call it that!) blends into its environment with its use of bare beams and adobe. The original building was the honeymoon cottage Orson Wells built for his bride, Rita Hayworth, in the '40's. And although the structure has been expanded greatly and now includes a two-story gift-and-handcraft shop, the entire complex remains totally unobtrusive and completely natural.

The food Nepenthe serves is created in the same vein. Simplicity is the keynote, and the finest quality is the accepted norm. As you laze on the outside terrace overlooking the massive coastline to the south, you will swear your Ambrosia Burger is the finest you have ever enjoyed. The kosher pickle crackles merrily under your bite and the bean salad positively beams with the joyousness of sprightly herbs. French fries must be ordered separately and are cooked to order. Even in the darkest dungeon, I would know they are the ultimate in fries—crispy, golden and irresistible. And what a delight to find tea (no tea bag, either!) as beautifully brewed as it would be in a Mayfair drawing room. Sit here awhile and sip in silence. Nepenthe is to be slowly savored. It is a unique place.

1:45 p.m. I am always loathe to leave Nepenthe, to quit its hold on my senses, to take leave of the peaceful mien radiated by the Big Sur regulars who gather here, using it as a social and cultural center. But . . . we must leave.

We are headed to one of the most mind-boggling displays of ostentatious power and wealth in America. The drive to Hearst's Castle proper covers less than 60 miles, most of it being curves and hills. It should take over 2 hours, depending on stops. Speaking of stops, an important one for those interested in the creativity of the Big Sur Colony, is the Coast Gallery, south of Nepenthe on the left.

As you approach San Simeon, you can spot the massive complex of buildings on the crest of a hill several miles off in the distance, looming above the countryside like some wild creation of mad King Ludwig of Bavaria. Your overnight lodgings lie about 6½ miles further south, but you may wish to pull into the Castle's tourist center in order to pick up a brochure on the history and contents of the place.

As of this writing, plans are underway to have tickets to any of the Castle's three tours available for purchase in advance through a statewide ticket agency. In order to avoid the disappointment of finding all tours sold out on the day of your visit, I urge you to call the Hearst Castle Information Office at (805) 927-4621 to ascertain where you can purchase tickets locally. The cost of your phone call and the minimal service charge on the tickets are a small price to pay for the convenience and protection against disappointment.

Failing to obtain your Hearst Castle tickets in San Francisco, you should purchase them at the Castle on the afternoon of your arrival for the earliest available tours the next morning.

As of this writing, there are three tours available. All tours are guided. No cars are allowed up at the Castle; you are bused there. Tour #1 includes the swimming pools, one guest house, the garden, and the ground floor of the Castle itself. Tour #2 shows you the pools, garden, upper level of the Castle and the kitchen. Tour #3 takes in the pools, garden and guest rooms of the North Wing. Tour #1 is recommended for all first-time visitors, but I found some of the rooms on Tour #2 extremely interesting, especially the Celestial Suite filled with an almost magical light created by the sun filtering through the filligree-carved shutters. Naturally, the kitchen holds a special place in my interests!

There is little reason for me to devote much time to details on the Castle or its contents. The complimentary brochure and your well-schooled guides will give you plenty of facts and figures. All I can and should say is that you are due for one of the most thrilling experiences of your life. I had many misconceptions about the Hearst San Simeon Castle. I had thought from my reading that all of it was grotesque and in poor taste. So I was in for a surprise when I first visited it. It contains some magnificent antiques, even if they are mixed with little regard for their aesthetic effect on one another, to say nothing of an utter disregard for chronology.

The most surprising thing, however, is that the Castle was not created as a stuffy museum but as the actual, comfortable residence of one man. I think this is the thing which astonishes tourists. Big, overstuffed, inexpensive and floral-covered chairs are scattered in rooms containing ceilings worth hundreds of thousands of dollars. This, too, comes up for much criticism on the part of interior decorators, but I do not agree. One must keep in mind that floral, overstuffed chairs were much in vogue in the days this Castle was being furnished and, whether they are in good taste or not, they certainly look comfortable and inviting. In fact, all the rooms look livable despite their inclusion of some startling antique pieces.

A trip to Hearst's Castle would be worth it for the outdoor swimming pool alone. I doubt if you will ever see anything like this again in American architecture. It is breathtakingly beautiful. Add to this the great variety of flowers and fruit trees which, incidentally, are especially magnificent in the spring, and you will have a two-hour tour you will never forget.

After stopping at the Castle's tourist center to pick up an illustrated brochure, simply continue further down Highway 1 for 6½ miles to Moonstone Beach Drive, turning right to San Simeon Pines (805) 927-4648. The Pines is by no means elegant or luxurious, but it is perfect for your one-night stay. The whole atmosphere is friendly and accommodating. An even greater plus is the fact that only a few yards away is a lovely seashore park, maintained by the state. Here you can shuffle aimlessly along the sandy beach, or sit up on the bluff among the cypress awaiting the descent of the sun into the vast Pacific. It is an ideal place to stretch your legs after the tension of the Highway 1 drive. (Closer to the Castle is the larger, more modern and box-like San Simeon Lodge, 805-927-4601.)

When you check into the Pines, ask the clerk to place a dinner reservation for you at whatever hour you wish at the Brambles, Burton Drive, Cambria (805) 927-4716. The Brambles is the kind of restaurant one hopes to uncover in out-of-the-way tourist spots, but seldom does. After all, here is an establishment catering primarily to one-time Castle visitors. The majority of restaurants which have this kind of captive, never-to-return clientele usually take advantage of the situation with poor food and non-existent service. Happily for you, the Brambles is a noteworthy exception. The menu is the plain, honest-to-goodness type with no frills. But the steaks and salmon (in season) are broiled to perfection over oak coals. The Clam Chowder is unusually tasty, and the breads are homemade. On one visit, both the onion bread and light-textured pumpernickel were delicious. If a restaurant takes the time and trouble to bake their own breads, one would expect out-of-the-ordinary baked desserts—and the Brambles' cheesecake was just that. Faultlessly swift and efficient service in this remote area makes me wonder all the more why so many city restaurants cannot come up with the same.

THE FOURTH DAY

Hopefully, you were able to purchase tickets to a fairly early morning tour of the Castle. So the best course of action is to pack up the car first, check out and head north to the Castle.

After you have witnessed Mr. Hearst's home and pondered a bit on the unfathomable wealth that allowed him to construct it, you are ready to end your excursion and to return to San Francisco. You do not have to face torturous Highway 1 again. There is a very simple route back. It will not give you the incredible scenic wonders of the Big Sur Coast, but its straight four-lane freeway construction certainly will be welcomed.

All you need do is exit left from the Castle's parking area, heading south on Highway 1. In 12½ miles, turn left again on Highway 46. After 20 miles of smooth, gradually graded roadway rising to some 1,700 feet above verdant farmlands, you will connect with Highway 101 North. In about 3½ to 4 hours, you will be back in San Francisco. However, the first one who says, "That Hearst Castle is a great place to visit, but I wouldn't want to live there" walks!

If, after your long drive back to San Francisco, you want to just settle for a room-service dinner in your hotel, I can't really blame you. I know the feeling all too well! On the other hand, because there was no scheduled lunch stop, a visit to another fine restaurant might be just the thing after a brief rest. And to fill that bill, I have two recommendations.

Orsi's, 375 Bush Street, (981-6535), is one of the city's most popular de luxe Italian restaurants. Its favorable location on the perimeter of the financial district helps insure a turn-away lunch business. At night, its expert Italianate handling of top quality ingredients attracts a regular following from all over the Bay Area, myself included. Over the years, I have distilled from Orsi's vast menu, the essence of their best—and this is what I will share with you now.

Without exception, I start my Orsi dinner with prosciutto (that paper-thin, pungent Italian ham), served with either fresh melon or fresh pears. Orsi's cures their own prosciutto, which may account for its exemplary moistness and delicacy. And when this auspicious ham is placed in tandem with vine-ripened melon or sugar-sweet pears, the combination is ambrosial. My next course is also preordained—sauteed scampi. Scampi are not prawns but rather crustaceans which sport five-petaled tails. And since the waters which immediately surround the U.S. do not support scampi, they must be imported frozen. In Venice, where they are indigenous, scampi can be simply grilled. This plain style of cooking, however, is not acceptable for frozen ones, so American chefs must discover other methods. And Orsi's has hit upon just about the finest sauteeing technique, calling upon a lemony wine sauce to bring out the scampi's intrinsic sweetness.

Like their prosciutto, Orsi's also makes their own fettucine, those fragile ribbons of egg pasta which, when judiciously enveloped in butter, cream and cheese, become food for the gods. Orsi's magical handling of this pasta compels me into ordering it as my main course. (You will notice that this paragon of Orsi's dinners contains no meat course, except the initial ham. If you must have more meat, I suggest you substitute Orsi's brilliant meat-filled cannelloni for the fettucine as a main course. In this way, you will not have to bypass some of their great homemade pasta.)

Then, a fine vinegary green salad is called for before Orsi's remarkable Cassata Siciliana, a homemade Sicilian cheesecake unmatched anywhere in the city. The perfect final touch to a perfect dinner.

One important color in San Francisco's incredibly varied palette of ethnic cuisines was brilliantly restored with the opening of Gaylord India Restaurant, Ghirardelli Square, (771-8822). San Francisco always has possessed a few Indian restaurants, but of recent years, their general quality seemed to deteriorate beyond consideration by those who admire this cuisine. The advent of Gaylord, however, initiated a renewed interest. And not only does this San Francisco branch of the international dining operation provide us with an awesome cross section of India's culinary styles, but it also displays them against an elegant background, devoid of the "kitchery" of turbans and flaming swords.

When I dine at Gaylord, I order my dinner served in several courses, similar to a Chinese meal. My two favorite first courses are Vegetable Pakora and Chicken Chatt. The former is related in concept to a Japanese tempura but the batter which surrounds the vegetable pieces in this dish is puffier, without any trace of oiliness. Dip them into the

yogurt-onion-mint sauce, as you would dip tempura into
soy sauce. If the pakora is the epitome of blandness, the
chicken chatt is cold in temperature but fiery hot in flavor,
the latter condition caused by the chili-pepper marinade.
After several tastings, it remains one of my favorite first
courses in all of San Francisco.

My next course is Tandoori Chicken, a northern Indian
preparation of roasting the marinated fowl in a special, extremely hot oven which seals in the juices. The tandoori technique can be witnessed in a Tandoori Mixed Grill, also.
Following the tandoori course, I proceed to a curried dish,
such as the Sag Gosht which weds lamb with minced spinach
and a host of spices. In the Lamb Pasanda, the meat is first
braised and then treated to a spiced yogurt sauce. As a
vegetable dish to accompany this course, I lean toward
Matter Paneer, cubelets of made-on-the-premises farmer's
cheese simmered with green peas in a delicious gravy.

There are several breads available (you can watch them
being baked in the glass-enclosed kitchen off the foyer),
and they range from a buttered whole wheat Paratha to a
puffy onion-speckled Nan. As one would expect from the
land of Darjeeling, various teas are offered and they are
properly brewed! As for my beverage with the meal, I have
never found wine congenial to Indian food but consider a
chilled imported beer the ideal partner. Oh, yes, Gaylord
features a complete vegetarian dinner and thus provides
persons who shun meat, fish and fowl with a superbly prepared meal within the confines of their chosen diet.

There is an Indian proverb which states, "If you would
be a king, you must eat like a king." Even if you harbor
no regal aspirations, your meal at Gaylord, Ghirardelli
Square, San Francisco, should make you feel very special.

Why Is San Francisco Such a Great Restaurant City?

WHEN IT COMES to the quality, sheer number and variety of restaurants, San Francisco ranks second only to New York City. But when one considers the entire "restaurant experience," no city in America, not even New York, rivals the City by the Bay. Why?

Because, quite simply, San Francisco is a *restaurant town*. Its residents consider "restaurant going" a cultural activity in the same way New Yorkers think of their theaters. Attend a typical party here and you find the conversation often dominated by references to the latest dining-out discovery, the loss of a famous chef by another establishment, or the deterioration of a previously highly regarded dining emporium.

We San Franciscans find it easy to go out to a restaurant. Distances are short and we think nothing of popping out to a low-rent residential area to try the latest entry into Moroccan or Vietnamese cooking. We are even willing to cross a bridge or journey down the Peninsula if we hear of a new and exciting addition to the restaurant scene. And we do all this secure in the knowledge we will not be greeted by haughty headwaiters with outstretched palms demanding a reward before granting us a table. We have little or no fear we will be subjected to snobby waiters. And with the possible exception of one (Trader Vic's), special preferred sections or rooms in our restaurants are not reserved for only the very rich, or the famous, or the regulars.

Add to this the exciting variety of ethnic foods being served and you have San Francisco—a restaurant-goer's paradise! Restaurants serving regional Chinese food other than Cantonese, such as Hunanese, Szechwan, Pekinese and

Shanghai, were known here long before their national popularity; authentic Moroccan restaurants here pioneered this exotic cuisine in America; a family-run Vietnamese restaurant opened here years before this kind of cooking was even presented in New York.

The San Francisco restaurant scene does have a few gaps. By and large, our seafood restaurants cannot compare with those of the East because the Pacific coast cannot compare with the Atlantic coast for aquatic produce; however, careful selection can go a long way to offsetting this limitation. Also, although we have three acceptable Jewish-type delicatessens in our theater district, none have found a way, as yet, to present the quality of hot pastrami and corned beef found only in New York.

Yet, unless you plan to hold a U.S. restaurant olympics and serve as judge, you are bound to find the entire restaurant-going experience in San Francisco more satisfying than that in any other American city. It is quite possibly the last remaining American city where you can approach your selection of restaurants with the warm feeling that you will be treated courteously, that your patronage will be welcomed, and the food you order will be, in most cases, unmatched elsewhere. There are exceptions, of course. But with the copy of this book you now hold in your hands, it is hoped you will follow my personal selections throughout and avoid them.

Index to Recommended Restaurants

This index covers all restaurants recommended in this book and, for your convenience, lists them by location and style of cuisine served. Because restaurants often change days and hours open, *you are urged to phone ahead in all cases*. And, except where they are not accepted, reservations are strongly advised. The description of the restaurant along with specific menu suggestions appear on the pages indicated in italics.

Recommended Restaurants:

Restaurants by Location:

San Francisco and Marin County Restaurants
by type of cuisine:

INDEX

Cover Design by Allan Friedman
Photography furnished by San Francisco Convention
& Visitors Bureau